Faith, Friends and Other Flotation Devices

a woman's guide to abundant living

Michele Howe

PUBLICATIONS

FAITH, FRIENDS AND OTHER FLOTATION DEVICES
A Woman's Guide to Abundant Living
by Michele Howe

Cover art and interior illustrations from Bigstock
Editing, design and typesetting by Patricia A. Lynch

Copyright © 2014 by Michele Howe

Published by ACTA Publications, 4848 N. Clark St.,
Chicago, IL 60640, (800) 397-2282, actapublications.com

Scripture texts in this work are taken from *The Message: The Bible in Contemporary Language (Catholic/Ecumenical Edition)*, © 2013 by Eugene Peterson. Used with permission of NavPress.

Library of Congress Catalog Number: 2014938752
ISBN: 978-0-87946-527-8
Printed in the United States of America by Total Printing Systems
Year 20 19 18 17 16 15 14
Printing 12 11 10 9 8 7 6 5 4 3 2

♻ Text printed on 30% post-consumer recycled paper

Contents

Introduction

God has blessed us with a three-strand, no-fail plan for navigating life's challenges. Can you guess the strands of this fundamental trio? It's fabulously simple.

- **Faith** — that personal, intimate relationship with Jesus that give us the hope of making an eternal difference by focusing completely on the faithfulness of God in ever-changing circumstances.
- **Friends** — those fun-loving, fiercely loyal women whose relationships stand the test of time and trial.
- **Flotation Devices** — the skills, experiences and wisdom of a fragrant, fruitful life nurtured by God.

Look around, and you'll see I'm right. Each and every day we women rely on our faith, our friends and a multitude of what I call flotation devices. God gives us a plentiful supply of resources to help us thrive: robust scriptural promises, intimate caring relationships, a generous supply of buoyant faith-filled, life-saving instruction. As we flourish, so do all those who come into contact with us.

"What is it that keeps me afloat?" The first purpose of this book is to help you answer this question. In other words, what holds you steady, keeps you on course, and helps you remain focused when all of life's stresses and demands threaten to pull you under? In each chapter, I offer an example of a woman who has faced down hardship, hurt and disappointment by banking on the truth found in God's word. I hope you will be encouraged by these examples to help you understand and cope with the demands in your own life. What better way to discover and appreciate God's intended purposes before, during and after each season of stretching and molding?

I also offer twenty "flotation devices" — faith-inspiring exercises at the end of each chapter — to help you apply God's life-giving truth in everyday situations. I hope you will see how faith, when embraced, is powerful indeed; how the right friends can serve as stalwart counselors to influence, guide and accompany you; and how surrendering your will through God's grace is truly the most freeing, peaceful and fruitful way to live.

In this book I use *The Message: Catholic / Ecumenical Edition* by Presbyterian minister and biblical scholar Rev. Eugene Peterson to help us uncover fresh meaning in the familiar verses of the Bible, that is, to hear God's word in a new and faith-affirming way.

Michele Howe
LaSalle, Michigan

Faith

It's what we trust in but don't yet see that keeps us going.
2 CORINTHIANS 5:7

*E*verywhere we look — billboards, magazines, newspapers, books, movies or television programs — we are bombarded with the message that what we *see* is what we get. Tempting as it can be to fall prey to this dangerous pressure — and it *is* tempting, God's word tells us to believe the very opposite. Clearly stated, the Bible commands us to "live by faith, not by sight." Can't get any clearer than that, can we? This directive makes marvelous sense — the faith-type-of-sense, that is — for the Bible tells us that we will have trouble in this world, but that Christ has overcome it — *all* of it.

Circumstances frequently weigh us down, burden us with their complexity, and confound us as we try to make sense of our lives. Sadly, we spend far too much time and effort trying to figure out "why?" and "how can I?" instead of leaning on the solid truths of Scripture. God's word can give us the strength to get past the daily distractions and to find healing for today's heartaches. After all, we are called to live by faith. Let's step past the need to see with our eyes and start focusing our attention on matters of the heart of faith.

Tuned In

Oblivious to the escalating demands placed upon her, Renee sat typing away on her computer, working against a looming deadline and rising blood pressure to complete her latest and, thankfully, final research paper.

Feeling the muscles in her upper back spasm again, Renee wondered for umpteenth time just how prudent a choice she'd made when she decided to finish her undergraduate degree in elementary education. It seemed as soon as she had enrolled, her life had gone into overdrive. And it had. Even though her two children were now college-age young adults, Renee and her husband Rick held active positions in several community volunteer organizations. Both were also caring for an elderly parent. Still, Renee was eager to complete her education and allow her long-held-at-bay dream of becoming a teacher take flight.

But neither Renee nor Rick had counted on his dad falling and breaking a hip and, at the same time, Renee's dad developing double pneumonia. She found herself running between the hospital and the nursing facility morning and afternoon. Trying to manage her home and doing double-duty at her father's house and her in-law's place was driving Renee to distraction.

Unable to concentrate, Renee pushed herself away from the desk and took a deep breath. And another.

"Relax," she chided herself. "You've faced worse before."

Glancing around the office, Renee spied the large conch shell she'd retrieved from last year's beach vacation. She picked it up, examined the rough, bleached exterior, and then held it to her ear. She could hear the faint sound of the ocean within.

Breathing more slowly now, Renee closed her eyes and remembered how she had relaxed on the beach every day, eyes shut to the rest of the world, and simply listened to the rush of waves. She'd felt so at peace and so secure knowing that the God who created such majesty was always watching over her, guarding her.

Yes, life right now was hard, and Renee's heart hurt to bursting, but she also realized she had to take responsibility for her own responses to the outside stresses. No one but she could take charge of her attitude and the direction she allowed her thoughts and emotions to travel.

Opening her eyes, Renee thanked God for the power such a memory held as it healed and sustained her even now.

When I was upset and beside myself,
you calmed me down and cheered me up.
PSALM 94:19

Truth, especially biblical truth, is like sand or oil. Like sand
it grinds at us, smoothing the rough places, causing friction
in our moving parts to get our attention and to halt certain
directions. Like oil, truth can smooth the rough ways of life,
soothe the hurts, and even heal the brokenhearted.
JERRY WHITE
MAKING PEACE WITH REALITY

Faith

when heartache happens

> *Nothing strengthens the judgment*
> *and quickens the conscience like individual responsibility.*
> ELIZABETH CADY STANTON

I hurt. You hurt. We all hurt. It's a given. At one time or another, we all feel the anguish of emotional pain. We are often emotionally driven, at the mercy of our ever-changing feelings, and far too dependent upon circumstances around us.

Clearly, some individuals express emotion more than others. But still, it is safe to say that all of us — every man, woman and child — experience the full gamut of emotional responses and will continue to do so our entire lives. It is our *reaction* to these powerful feelings that counts. Are we more reactive or proactive? Do we take some measure of responsibility for how we feel or not?

Most times, we respond to life's stresses — the ups and downs of daily living and any accompanying negative feelings — with an unconscious acceptance of both the good and bad. We realize that every day isn't going to be a warm-fuzzy-feeling one. On those especially wondrous occasions when every aspect of our emotional being affirms that life is good, we bask in a warm glow of satisfaction. Fleeting as those rare moments may be, we can mistakenly use them as the gauge and end goal for every other feeling we experience. If it makes us feel good, it must be good. If something makes us feel bad, it must be bad.

Not so, say Elyse Fitzpatrick and Laura Hendrickson, M.D., authors of *Will Medicine Stop the Pain?* Feeling bad can be a blessing in that it alerts us that something is wrong. We need to heed that warning and take action. Warnings, after all, are necessary and good.

Likewise, we can mistakenly believe that we are helpless victims of our volatile emotional state. Buying into this fatalistic mentality is never conducive to good health. Might it be more productive and more helpful if we start fighting against the blue moods with deliberate, vigorous attitude adjustments and lifestyle choices? We *can* learn to think differently. We *can* develop methods to approach our circumstances and our responses with grit and faith-fueled determination. By doing so, we can begin rewiring our automatic negative reactions and replace them with a change-is-possible outlook.

Fitzpatrick and Hendrickson also offer some reliable, practical thoughts on dealing with run-away emotions. For example, when feeling overwhelmed by feelings of discouragement, depression, or a simple case of downheartedness, we should become students of our own habits and circumstances: lifestyle choices, medication, fluctuating hormones, and attitudes toward life in general. We should learn what triggers affect our moods, and train ourselves to anticipate those events, situations or people that historically bring emotional upset. Then we should take responsibility for making internal or external changes. Perception matters. Choices matter. So instead of giving in to the blues, we should counter them with constructive, decisive thinking and action. It's surprising how these bleak emotions can slowly be replaced by a positive outlook. Do it for you, do it for others.

FAITH-FUELED EXERCISES
FOR YOUR EMOTIONS

- Be your own detective. Recognize the areas where you tend to struggle most and be ready to prevent emotional derailments.
- Fight emotional angst by giving thanks. Give thanks for at least ten things every morning.
- Meditate on the truth. Locate and memorize Bible passages that speak of God's promises to provide and care for us.
- Take the offensive. Talk back to yourself when you start to feel overwhelmed or defeated.
- Pray daily for the mind of Christ. Ask God for wisdom and insight on every matter.

Friends

"This is the very best way to love.
Put your life on the line for your friends."
JOHN 15:13

There isn't a single time in our lives when we don't need the fellowship, encouragement and accountability of good friends. Whether times are flush with happiness and over-flowing with success of every sort or filled with paralyzing, incapacitating fear, we all need those emotional buffer zones that only other women can provide. Given the pace at which we live our lives, we have to make room, clear out space, and give precedence to time with our friends. The companionship of other women — young or old — is an absolute requirement for a healthy life.

It is within the confines of these trustworthy, loyal friendships that we learn best how to celebrate joyfully, wait patiently, endure hardship with courage, mourn our losses, and govern our responsibilities with maturity and poise. We are all learners as well as teachers. Whom will we choose to teach or guide us? In whom will we invest? For whom will we lay down our lives? And to whom will we impart that precious store of knowledge that has been given to us? From one friend to another, we pass on life through our perspectives, our example and our faith.

Eye Opener

"Got one!" yelled Virginia.

"Me, too!" called another.

"Look at all I have!" chimed in yet another. "I was smart. I brought along my own net."

Virginia laughed. "Think we have enough now? Come here, ladies," she invited. "Let's join ranks. Okay, now, guide them into my jar...carefully, carefully. We don't want to injure them."

"Oh yeah, what would that look like, a bunch of old women running around in the dark, capturing lightning bugs only to mercilessly kill them?" one joked.

Virginia smiled broadly. "Look! The jar is now alight with fireflies."

Placing the hole-punctured lid on top of the oversized glass pickle jar, Virginia set the living centerpiece in the middle of the table.

"Ooh, how pretty," cooed Karen, Virginia's partner in setting up these silly schemes. "Turn the deck lights down low, will you? Fascinating, all those little flies with their tails alight...it's beautiful."

After gazing for a few more moments, Virginia got everyone settled at the picnic table and then brought out refreshments — iced tea sprigged with fresh lemon slices, freshly-squeezed lemonade, and an assortment of fruits, cheeses, spreads and crackers. One paper plate after another was passed around. Next came the plastic flatware and finally the napkins.

"Dessert to follow, ladies," Virginia announced.

As the women sat comfortably, munching on their snacks, they spoke of times gone by. Some now were widowed, a couple never married, one was divorced, but all were comrades at heart.

A few summers back, Virginia and Karen decided on the spur of the moment to work harder at getting the ladies together more often. With all the life changes they were experiencing, the stresses of growing families, and even the unexpected events, Virginia realized that they'd become so busy that they no longer had the time or opportunity to share their trials and joys.

"Have to remedy that," Karen said decisively after Virginia brought up her disappointment. On this particular occasion, Karen and Virginia decided a lightning bug hunt was just the ticket to an evening of fun, laughter and friendship.

Every time I think of you — and I think of you often! — I thank God for your lives of free and open access to God, given by Jesus. There's no end to what has happened in you — it's beyond speech, beyond knowledge.
1 CORINTHIANS 1:4-5

*He met us where we were
and crowned us with love and compassion.*
JUD WILHITE
FAITH THAT GOES THE DISTANCE

Friends

the art

of appreciation

> *The difference between appreciation and flattery? That is simple. One is sincere and the other insincere. One comes from the heart out; the other from the teeth out.*
> DALE CARNEGIE
> HOW TO WIN FRIENDS & INFLUENCE PEOPLE

Isn't it wonderful when another person notices your efforts, weak attempts though they may be, and kindly expresses such recognition with even *a single word* of thankfulness? Just one paltry word? Yes, a single word can make or break a person's spirit. Depend on it. Even if we can't identity our need, we all — male and female, young and old, from every background — have an inner longing for a bit of expressed good will. We all have a need to be validated for our accomplishments, our purpose and our very being. Not to be *flattered*, but to be *appreciated*. Some say there's a fine line between appreciation and flattery, but flattery is obviously verbal manipulation that benefits the one doing the flattering. The words may true or not, but that's not the point.

Appreciation runs deeper. It takes note of another person and sees the good in the person's actions, attitude, or words — no matter how insignificant. Real appreciation changes both the speaker and the recipient for the good. It renews our vision, encourages continued effort, and lights a fire for ongoing perseverance toward excellence.

Perhaps the most significant difference between flattery and appreciation is that appreciation offers life in abundance while flattery falls flat. People instinctively know if they're being celebrated or schmoozed.

The challenge, then, is how to offer genuine praise when someone seems to be lacking or undeserving. Ralph Waldo Emerson once wrote, "Every man I meet is my superior in some way, and in that, I learn from him." Wise words and utterly true. We need to find a reason to acknowledge the goodness in *everyone* we meet.

As we practice the art of identifying strength and goodness in the people we meet and offer words of genuine appreciation, we will take part in their success, which will naturally spill over, positively affecting countless others. Begin today by focusing on the strong points of the people in your life and make a commitment to communicate sincere appreciation every day. A few powerful words, which cost us so little, will long be treasured by the recipients, even when we've long forgotten what we've said. There's nothing insincere about it.

- Adopt a learner's mentality. View every person — friends and strangers alike — as someone who can teach you something.
- Focus on meeting the needs of others by learning what is important to them. Ask intelligent questions, listen carefully to their responses, and spend more time discussing your friends' interests than your own.
- See people with fresh eyes. Familiarity can dull our awareness and sense of appreciation. Look closely at others' gifts, talents and abilities. Thank them for the difference they are making in your life and in the lives of others.
- Be open-hearted by sharing friendships. Warmly welcome newcomers into your circle of friends and acquaintances. Genuine hospitality begins in each individual heart and works its way outward in ever-widening circles.

Balance

*Tell those rich in this world's wealth to quit being
so full of themselves and so obsessed with money,
which is here today and gone tomorrow.*
1 TIMOTHY 6:17

hy is it so difficult for us Christians to enjoy ourselves? Why do we feel guilty or ashamed when we take time off to simply have a little fun? It might be the way we were raised: No fun allowed until all the work is done. Honestly, whenever is all the work done? For us women especially, the to-do list is ever growing and never ending. And yet, while God's word tells believers not to chase after or put their trust in wealth, it does say God gives us — meaning *every one of us* — everything for our enjoyment. That means nature, pets, people, food, music, literature, theater, you name it — all things richly for us to enjoy. Our five senses were given to us for good reason (and within reason). God's created world is rife with opportunities to explore and experience these enjoyments firsthand. So, as we put our hope in God, we can — and should — enjoy the blessings too.

Clear Vision

Jane sat next to her two visiting aunts as they took an hour-long boat tour down the river just south of her home. On either side of the river, the scenery was breathtaking. Gorgeous riverfront properties and dream houses lined the steeply sloped land. Just beyond the immediate landscape, Jane could see the tops of the mountains, *her* mountains. Even though all this was close to home, she was taken aback, in awe at the picturesque setting surrounding her on all sides. Always a lover of beautifully designed homes, she was captivated by what she was studying.

Her aunts were obviously relishing the ride as well. Jane listened to the two of them casually bantering back and forth, estimating the cost of the spectacular homes before them.

After awhile Jane began to grow irritated with their conversation as it took a more personal turn. They talked about how grand it would be to live in such palaces and have the resources to enjoy all the perks that went along with living there.

Jane, having struggled financially her entire adult life, found her joy in the day had vanished. Always one to look for the reason behind events, she realized she was no longer admiring the lush scenes around her. Instead she was envying those who lived lives she could scarce imagine.

"I've worked hard, harder than most I know," Jane reminded herself. "Didn't I take on two jobs when we were first married? Didn't I continue to work after the children went back to school? I was always at the ready when someone needed assistance, and I volunteered more times than I care to recall."

Jane's mood had taken a detour right along with her train of thought.

Hearing her aunts suddenly laugh made her jump. Shaking off her dark humor, she stopped considering what she *couldn't* have and started recounting all she *did* possess.

"I've got a husband who loves me. Two terrific kids. Assorted dogs, cats and an awful excuse for a hamster," she mused. "A home that we own. And the best view in town...majestic mountains right outside my kitchen window. What more could I ask?"

Everything God created is good,
and to be received with thanks.
Nothing is to be sneered at and thrown out.
1 Timothy 4:4

The spigot of blessing will always, at some point, run dry. It is simply false teaching to say otherwise. God does bless those who obey him, but not always with such blessing as many erroneously teach. His ultimate desire is that we know him. It is a scanty "knowing" that comes by blessing alone.
Michael Phillips
Make Me Like Jesus

Balance

vices and virtues

> *Every voluntary act of a man's life*
> *is either virtuous or vicious.*
> LYSANDER SPOONER, 1875

There are virtues (the good guys), and then there are vices (the bad guys). But who's to say which is which? Do we rely on circumstance to distinguish between the two? Are the lines separating right and wrong so elastic that they change given our situation, mood or disposition? Sometimes our choices shift hour-by-hour as we go to work, feed our pets, parent our children, shop for clothing, and watch the evening news. In other words, we act in order to create a happy or purposeful life, but we can err by investing too much time, energy (emotional, physical and mental), and material resources on specific projects, single goals, objects, or people, so much so that the rest of our lives are thrown out of whack.

Can any of the above responsible activities can be measured as vices? Well, sure they can. Anything, even a good endeavor, taken to extremes, can become a personal idol which controls and masters us. Does this include activities such as working, cleaning, mowing the lawn, or running errands for a neighbor? Yes, it does. Unless we make a deliberate effort to keep everything in balance, our lives can quickly spin out of control. Too much of something is simply too much.

Even if we find satisfaction in lending a hand or offering our services unreservedly, we sometimes need to ask the difficult questions: Is what I'm doing benefiting or handicapping another (or myself) in the long run? Am I shortchanging another (or myself) by putting this much emphasis on a particular activity, person or vocational goal?

A good way to determine whether a specific act falls into the vice or virtue column is to look at the degree of commitment. How do we do this? By continually reassessing our lives — within reason, of course. We need to reflect on how we spend our hours and days and be willing to pull back in those areas where we are choking the life out of others and ourselves. Give and take…balance, balance, balance. In all things, strive for balance.

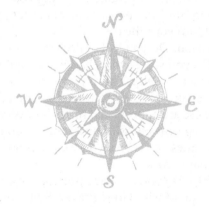

- **Work.** Do you weary yourself out to gain riches? The Bible says that's foolish. Do a self-check and take a long hard look at what motivates you to work hard. Is it financial gain? Acceptance from peers? Success as its own end? Now consider how much your life might become richer by bringing this area into real balance.

- **Rest.** Do you take some time every day for rejuvenation? What about following the Bible's injunction to rest on the Sabbath? Do you struggle against the very idea of taking time off from being productive, not recognizing that perhaps the most productive thing you can do in the long run is to incorporate consistent spaces of rest into your life every day?

- **Recreation.** Do you feel guilty when you have fun? Do you secretly feel bad when you're enjoying yourself because you know others are suffering or doing without? Remember, the Bible says there are appropriate times for everything, including times for simply having a good time. These times are as blessed by God as doing a good day's work.

- **Worship.** Do you set aside portions of every day to spend with God? Prayer, Bible study, and meditation all bring needed perspective and balance to our lives. We need God's inspired word to instruct us, renew us and encourage us…and we need this powerful spiritual practice daily.

Forgiveness

Be even-tempered, content with second place,
quick to forgive an offense.
Forgive as quickly and completely
as the Master forgave you.
Colossians 3:13

*M*emories that stay with us the longest are the ones attached to the most powerful emotions. When we experience positive feel-good emotions — happiness, gratitude, thankfulness, pure joy, we remember even the smallest details associated with them. On the flip side, we also remember negative emotions — rejection, stinging remarks, callous criticism, or condemnation — with similar clarity. Those uplifting memories can buoy us up and keep us emotionally afloat for weeks and months. Sadly, even fleeting reminders of those times when we were wronged can drag us down into a sea of bitterness and unforgiveness. We sometimes internalize these wrongs and stew over them endlessly.

We pay a higher price for clutching our anger and resentment than we do surrendering our hurts to the Lord and letting God be the one who vindicates. The Bible admonishes us to bear with one another — even when others offend us, when they sin against us willfully — and forgive them, remembering how all encompassing God's forgiveness was for us. Offering forgiveness is not pain-free, but obedience to Christ has its own greater reward: the freedom and peace and blessed relinquishment that come with trusting in God to see things righted in his time and in his way.

Basics

Victoria thumbed her way through three hairstyle magazines before she found one that suited. "Something simple, easy to maintain, and something that will work with my unruly hair. Is that too much to ask?" she wondered.

Given several months of change at home and at her workplace, Victoria had made enough concessions for a lifetime. And she realized the biggest alteration was yet to come. In five short weeks, Victoria would officially be a divorced woman. It pained her to even go there. All the hows and what-ifs were still in the back of her mind, but she now she spent her mental energy contemplating how to survive both emotionally and financially.

Victoria continued to relive the emotional counterplay she'd endured when her husband said he was moving out that weekend. Stunned and in disbelief, she tried to talk him out of it, suggested counseling, or even going away for a while to regroup, but all in vain.

Eventually recognizing defeat, Victoria got herself into counseling and continued to work through her anger and bitterness. She couldn't believe how exhausted she'd become. Each night after work, she'd literally drag herself through the door and crash on the couch. Then, after a restless night, she'd force herself back out the door and head to work.

Weeks went by as Victoria clung to this pitiful pattern until a friend stopped over and made Victoria accompany her to the symphony. She had to admit it had done her good. One small step led to others, and finally she was taking it upon herself to schedule needed — and wanted — appointments.

Today was one such engagement. Victoria was actually looking forward to bending her head back over the rinse sink and shutting her eyes for a bit to savor the pampering as she used to do. It wouldn't take her long to relax in the capable hands of her friendly stylist. Then she'd be ushered to a quieter corner where could relax while sipping a juice concoction and listening to the gentle sounds of an artisan's metal waterfall. This was the best part, Victoria believed — relishing a small sliver of time as her outer shell was shaped up and her soul was rejuvenated. She was well aware that there was no more appropriate period in her life to take advantage of these measures of kindness, each reminding her of God's tender graces still at work in the world.

God's readiness to give and forgive is now public. Salvation's available for everyone! We're being shown how to turn our backs on a godless, indulgent life, and how to take on a God-filled, God-honoring life. This new life is starting right now, and is whetting our appetites for the glorious day when our great God and Savior, Jesus Christ, appears.
TITUS 2:11-13

Dragons and nits and the noonday demons lie in wait. But the road is not entirely rough. There are oases along the way. It would be a dreadful mistake to assume that our Beloved is only waiting for us at the end of the road. Our communion with him sustains us along our path.
BRENT CURTIS AND JOHN ELDREDGE
THE SACRED ROMANCE

Forgiveness

framing our hurts

> *A frame is what you put around a picture*
> *to give it perspective.*
> DR. DICK TIBBITS
> *FORGIVE TO LIVE*

How big is your frame? Large or small? Ever considered that the way we view an offense is like a picture frame? Interesting concept isn't it? When we feel hurt (justified or not), we frame the experience within our hearts and minds. There we're likely to recall it, run the event over in our minds, sometimes complete with hand wringing and other dramatics. Sadly, the more we focus on the painful interchange, the more out of balance and skewed it becomes. The color goes blurry. We forget how much we used to appreciate the big picture, how it often brought us pleasure and comfort.

Dr. Dick Tibbits, author of *Forgive to Live*, says this: "A small frame focuses your attention on a very specific aspect of the total picture, while a larger frame allows you to see a much more comprehensive scene." In other words, when someone injures us, the actual size of the offense (big or small) doesn't make one whit of difference. We blow it out of proportion. We feel wounded. We feel betrayed. We feel misunderstood. We feel wronged, perhaps even justly so. Yet according to Tibbits, it really doesn't matter what another does to us. It's our response that counts.

How we choose to frame our life interactions will determine the story we tell. When we select a small frame, we narrow our perspective. When we opt for a larger frame, we get a wider perspective. So what's the advantage of making a deliberate choice to reframe our hurts by placing them in the context of our larger story? Tibbits believes that as we choose to be big-picture people, we will be better able to handle life's unfairness and injustices. Our frame will be so large that no single event can ruin the picture. That is, the more expansive the frame of reference, the more we will be able to see the negative encounter through a wider lens that tells us this isn't the end of our life story. Somehow, simply making this one choice, we become victors instead of hapless victims. And since we all know that rain — including negative encounters with people — falls on both the good and bad, preparing ahead of time is prudent and wise.

Dr. Tibbits's Reframing Tips

- Focus on what is true from both points of view.
- Develop empathy for the one who hurt you.
- Identify the wrongs you have committed that need forgiving.
- Revise your story so it more accurately reflects all points of view.
- Imagine your desired outcome and make adjustments toward that end.
- Realize that forgiveness takes time. Almost never is it a one-time event.

Focus

And that's about it, friends. Be cheerful.
Keep things in good repair. Keep your spirits up.
Think in harmony. Be agreeable.
2 CORINTHIANS 13:11

Are you a wanderer? Or do you consider yourself to be focused, on the mark, and heading toward a specific goal? It's so easy to drift into aimlessness after a season of overwork, heartache or discouragement. Too easy, really. But God's word tells us to aim for something — for perfection. Now, don't allow the word *perfection* to derail you. This word implies working toward maturity, completion and excellence in character. God desires that we take aim by listening carefully to his mandates, by seeking unity with one another, and by being peaceable in order that God's peace and love will flow through us. Let's live today with a single focus in mind, that of resting in the comfort of God's promises to protect, provide and guide no matter where we find ourselves.

Wanderings

Grabbing her roommate Carrie's binoculars, Julie was determined. For the first time since she'd moved west, she set her mind on climbing the desert hills on the outskirts of town. Donning some comfortable clothes and tying the thick laces of her hiking boots, she was ready.

A short drive down the never-ending dusty highway and Julie arrived. Locking her car, she perused the area and checked the imposing wooden path markers. Which one to take? As was her norm of late, she was ambivalent, but finally decided on the shortest route to the top. Looking at her watch purely out of habit, she mused, "I'm not in a hurry today, but why waste time, right?" Putting one foot in front of the other, she started her ascent.

"This isn't so grand," Julie thought. "What's the fuss all about? Just keep climbing or Carrie will have to drag me up herself."

Step by step, Julie trudged, making the slow upward journey. Soon she became tired and stopped for a break. After about thirty minutes of climbing, her thoughts started to stray back toward what she had left at the bottom. The job that she loved, or did she? Her church, where she was way over-committed. Her boyfriend, the one who couldn't decide whether he wanted in or out of their relationship. Julie's heart and mind stung with the realization that she'd been living out these last few years by rote. Doing what she thought was right, but without any direction. If she were truly honest, she'd have to admit she was going in circles much of the time.

Stopping for another breather and turning to take in the entire city from her new vantage point, Julie gasped in delight. "There's so much out there. So this is what I've been missing!"

Feeling regret for the many months of wasted time, Julie had a small, but meaningful, epiphany. "I wonder," she thought, "how many other treasures I've missed for lack of vision? Carrie was right, getting outside has helped clear my mind, and it's renewed my resolve to take a deeper look at the direction my life's going."

"Thanks, friend," Julie spoke across the wind to Carrie as she turned back to the path to continue upward.

"But principled people hold tight, keep a firm grip on life,
sure that their clean, pure hands
will get stronger and stronger!"
Job 17:9

Many areas of our lives are productive and prosperous, yet
we've never felt so spiritually withered. Our calendars are
full, but our souls are empty.
Donald S. Whitne
Simplify Your Spiritual Life

Focus

finding direction

> *Whenever you exit planet Earth, your grave will bear a marker of time — a tombstone or memorial plaque. What is found on most? The dates of your birth and death. Life is what happens in the "dash" between the two.*
> DAVID H. MCKINLEY
> THE SEARCH FOR SATISFACTION

Where are you heading? Do you know? Have you made plans for the upcoming years? The next twelve months? This week? Today? Important questions deserve adequate time and attention. Without goals, preferably written goals, our dreams frequently die a quick death at the first sign of opposition or the slightest, most incidental setback.

We all know people whose dreams are routinely larger than life. These individuals are usually over the top with excitement and enthusiasm, and are enthralled with the idea of their future success. It may be amusing to watch their theatrics, but if we're honest, we're usually skeptical. We've witnessed the same song and dance too many times before. Even if we disguise our skepticism and cynicism, we may have a difficult time sharing their excitement or affirming their plans.

History and personal experience teach us that the individuals (and nations) who take careful account of their gifts, talents, abilities, resources and limitations are the ones who most often achieve their objectives. Sure, there are setbacks, risks and sacrifices, but when we know our destination, these wrinkles can be ironed out. After all, the end goal (written in black in white, remember) is an ever-present reminder of what is at stake.

David McKinley writes, "Life reflects design, sequence, and order." That is, finding practical ways to work toward our goal means firmly grasping reality with one hand while balancing in the other the most hopeful of possibilities. McKinley asks, "Are you living 'on purpose,' or have you given your life over to the random acts of occurrence — wishing, hoping, and yearning?" Good question.

ACHIEVING YOUR GOALS

- Make a five-year plan. Dream big, but put your dream and plan on paper for continued reflection. Do not be afraid to tweak the plan. Expect to do so.
- Accurately assess the pluses which include all personal (and financial) abilities, skills, talents, education and experience.
- Be realistic about limitations, including past shortfalls and mistakes. Pay close attention to situations that are difficult or undesirable. No repeat offenders allowed!
- Ask for input from others who are where you want to be. Invite the counsel of trusted friends, family and colleagues on a regular basis.
- Do the necessary research, stay current, and keep the plan in the forefront of your mind while attending to the small daily steps in between.
- Never give up. Expect opposition; don't run from it. Adopt the mindset of student. That is, be open to learning from every situation.

Providence

And this is just how my regime has been,
for God guaranteed his covenant with me,
Spelled it out plainly
and kept every promised word —
My entire salvation,
my every desire.

2 SAMUEL 23:5

Isn't it a wondrous thing to know God promises that our lives will blossom and bear fruit? Despite our lack of ability, lack of faithfulness, lack of energy? Yes, in spite of our shortcomings, God *can* and *will* provide all that we need to fulfill our responsibilities today. And as God works to conform us to the image of Christ, both in character and in service, we will grow more fruitful in many ways. Imagine the possibilities of surrendering our days and nights to God, confident that, regardless of our pain-laced past, our failures, our current struggles, God will provide a bountiful harvest. A harvest characterized by the fruit of the Spirit — "...love, joy, peace, patience, kindness, goodness, faithfulness, gentleness and self-control." That thought is enough reason to get up in the morning. Simply watch God work!

Fruitopia

Lois had been anxious about her tomatoes and the luncheon she had promised her neighbor as soon as her red tomatoes ripened.

As far back as Lois could remember, she had grown flavorful tomatoes in her backyard. It was her one gardening ritual and her single green-thumb success story. Friends used to tease her that if they wanted to get rid of a plant, they'd simply ask Lois to plant-sit for a week. Her dreary track record became an ongoing joke. Not so for tomatoes.

When Lois transferred to a city at an altitude she claimed could give one a nosebleed, she wondered if she'd ever enjoy her one solitary gardening triumph again. It was difficult enough to move so far away from everyone dear to her, let alone give up all the quaint charms that had been part and parcel of her life.

Lois had decided to plant a window box as soon as the last frost was history. Though she now lived in an apartment, she was determined to bring some creature comforts to her new home — to bring something outdoorsy and wild into her now sterile environment. She had gingerly pressed the seedlings into the rich soil. She had given them a good soaking and had been diligent in her daily care.

At first, Lois had been excited. The plants were growing and seemed to be thriving. Then, an unexpected chill did the tender plants in. Not to be daunted by one mishap, she had replanted. This time the weather had cooperated, but some unfamiliar insect had a hey-day on most of the leaves. Lois had checked with the local nursery, sprayed her tomato shoots and prayed for the best.

Every morning and evening Lois had peered out her kitchen window, eyeballing the progress of her plants...or lack thereof. In a couple of weeks, she had finally spotted several tiny green tomatoes. At last!

As they grew plump and rosy, Lois was jubilant. "I cannot believe I'm this excited about a few tomatoes." But she was.

When the big day arrived to harvest her fruit, Lois had been giddy. Although the picking wasn't anything compared with her previous harvests, it was a start. She had tenderly washed and dried each tomato before placing all of them carefully on her windowsill.

Now, after spending a day in the kitchen, she called her friend, inviting her over for the finest homemade tomato bread and pizza imaginable.

My choice is you, GOD, first and only.
And now I find I'm your choice!
You set me up with a house and yard.
And then you made me your heir!
PSALM 16:5-6

Never hold anything in reserve. Pour yourself out, giving the best that you have, and always be poor. Never be diplomatic and careful with the treasure God gives you.
OSWALD CHAMBERS
MY UTMOST FOR HIS HIGHEST

Providence

giving and receiving in abundance

> *Good, better, best; never let it rest*
> *till your good is better and your better is best.*
> ANONYMOUS

What difference does that little bit extra make? Does it count? Can you measure it? Bottle it? Afraid you won't be able to keep pace with it once you've demonstrated your finest stuff?

Asked another way, can any one of us really tell if we've given our all or maybe fudged a bit and only meted out a decent or respectable day's effort? Who can accurately say if we have put in the additional time, effort and attention required to tip the scales beyond mediocrity? In truth, only *we* can.

We all know if we've done our level best. When we go that extra mile, we feel good knowing we've exceeded expectations. Who doesn't appreciate that feeling following a job well done? Even adding a mere two percent more can make a world of difference on the job, at home and anywhere we decide to invest ourselves — a hobby, a volunteer position, a genuine friendship.

For any hard-headed, crunch-the-numbers, cynical types out there who decry the notion that no one really pays attention to that extra couple of percent, let's take at a look at a practical example. Say a young person starts out with an investment of $500 at 10% interest compounded monthly from age 7 to age 18. At age 18 that young person would have $1,495. By age 62, this amount would grow to $119,589, and by age 72, it would amount to $323,733. Nice return over the long haul. Now let's take the same initial investment and change only one factor. Instead of 10% interest, let's up the ante to 12% — a two percent increase. Given the same time frames, the initial $500 would be worth $1,859 at age 18; $355,694 at age 62; and finally, $1,173,928 at age 72. Note the difference! Note the principle: Give a little, get a little. Give a little more (or a lot), get a whole lot more.

It truly is the *little* things that can make a big difference. When we make a habit of pursuing excellence, our extra investment of time and talent will naturally spill over, multiply and advance any project or purpose. I'm not just talking about monetary returns. Since when did money mean more than quality of life, inner satisfaction, and a good conscience? Never did, never will. So at day's end, give it your all, and you'll be able to mark the day as one well spent and wisely invested.

- **P — persistence.** The midpoint of any project or problem is the most difficult juncture to get past. Remember that no effort is considered a failure if you give it your best.
- **E — excellence.** Too often we compete with one another when we should be competing solely against our own previous standards. Since no two of us begin at exactly the same starting point, it's not sensible to measure ourselves against the successes or failures of others.
- **R — resistance.** Expect and accept that there will be detours and roadblocks along the way. Plan for them. Don't let these obstacles derail you. Prepare to work around and through them.
- **C — consistency.** Every day do one task toward meeting your goal. Large or small, doesn't matter. It's the daily exercise of moving along your trajectory that counts.
- **E — energy.** Take good care of yourself so that you have the stamina to withstand the emotional and physical demands required to stay the course.
- **N — never give up.** Setbacks, drawbacks and discouragement will come, and your goal may change along the way. Make a commitment to finish what you've begun no matter what comes.
- **T — thankfulness.** Every day find ten reasons for gratitude. It can help to speak your list out loud, even if only to yourself.

Freedom

And when God is personally present, a living Spirit,
that old, constricting legislation is recognized as obsolete.
We're free of it! All of us!
2 CORINTHIANS 3:17

Inner freedom is God's gift to us. It is most keenly felt in that deep sigh of relief we experience as we discover how to exhale tension and stress, as well as how to let go of our tendency to over-commit, over-volunteer and over-work over the long haul. What does it take to reach that place of balance where we realize our efforts will not be the saving of anyone, any project, any plan, at any time? It takes time, some humbling moments, bumps and bruises, and even betrayal by those we trust.

Whether we are spending our days and hours working in the home, outside of it for pay, or as a volunteer, we eventually have to choose *for* or *against* our options, that is, to *say yes* or to *say no* to numerous opportunities that come our way. By learning to be selective, even in serving, we will have more to give and be better able to handle those carefully chosen responsibilities with more social, emotional, and physical skill and strength.

With Christ as our guide, we have the responsibility to make wise choices about how we will spend our time; in whom we will invest our skills, talents and gifts; and how we will interact with those around us. Freedom, received as a precious gift, must be handled with thoughtful care.

Spinners

When the alarm went off, Jenny was already tense. She had been up late the night before helping her son review his science report. Due this morning, of course. Whenever she didn't get enough sleep or had too little alone time, Jenny grew a tad surly. So it was no surprise to the rest of her family when she curtly announced that breakfast and lunches were an every-man-woman-and-child-for-themselves affair that morning.

No one argued. They just tiptoed around the kitchen while Jenny started gathering her things and ticking off items on her do-not-forget list. Delivering the sixteen poinsettias to her church was her top priority. She need to get them there well before the Christmas luncheon being hosted by the ladies auxiliary. How she got roped into heading up the decorating committee was still a mystery. Jenny groaned and grunted — perhaps a bit too noticeably — as she loaded her SUV, said a zippy good-bye, and headed out.

No sooner had Jenny put her car in reverse did she realize that the snow that had accumulated overnight and the gusty winds were going to slow her down. She carefully backed out of the driveway, determined to make it to church before her plants succumbed to the frigid air. Driving along, she continued to fight the tension building deep within. She took one deep breath, then another and another without any noticeable effect. She was still on edge.

As she continued along her favorite stretch of highway, the one that offered her such a magnificent view of the ocean, she caught herself trembling. "It's just been *too* hectic lately," she complained. "When will I learn to say no? I try and try to get us all on a more reasonable schedule but nothing works. All my beginning-of-the-year resolutions certainly haven't amounted to much. I'm still way over-committed and rarely have a night at home with my family. Not that they'd even be there! Another thoroughly depressing thought."

"Lord," Jenny prayed, "help me find a way to slow my pace. I can't take much more. You know I'm on the edge. Tell me what I can do to bring us back to hearth and home."

"Stop."

"Now?"

"Now."

Pulling over at the next overlook, Jenny for once obeyed that inner voice calling her to forego the urgent for the sake of the divine. From inside her vehicle she looked at the water cresting below and at the snow swirling around in its own private dance. Finally she felt a long-overdue calm taking residence in her heart.

"You wear yourselves out trying the new and the different,
and never see what a waste it all is.
You've always found strength for the latest fad,
never got tired of trying new religions."
ISAIAH 57:10

Most sins are ungodly exaggerations of things that are good.
EDWARD T. WELCH
WHEN PEOPLE ARE BIG AND GOD IS SMALL

Freedom

making the best use of a work day

> *For most people, earning a living is not an option;*
> *it's a requirement.*
> KATHERINE CROWLEY AND KATHI ELSTER
> *WORKING WITH YOU IS KILLING ME*

Even before the morning alarm goes off, when we are probably drifting somewhere in that twilight state between blissful slumber and being fully awake, we may already be dreading the next eight to twelve hours. Most of us are hard-working, responsible women who want to give it our all. We long to achieve vocational, volunteer and personal goals, and have committed ourselves to following through on our short- and long-term assignments. Still, we may feel overwhelmed, overlooked or just plain fed-up. Any prospects of finding inner satisfaction, fulfillment and purpose at the workplace, on the home front, or any other front may have been greatly reduced or died out.

At one time work and volunteer duties didn't demand much more than putting in eight hours at the daily grind in exchange for a paycheck. That equation has shifted significantly. We now demand a higher level of personal satisfaction for our paid or volunteer work. While we all desire an ideal work situation, few of us ever find it.

According to Katherine Crowley and Kathi Elster, authors of *Working with You Is Killing Me*, today's workers and volunteers are partly to blame for the state of things. Every workplace has its unique culture, flowing, in part, from its workers. How we recognize, identify and learn to handle the often-tricky interpersonal relationships is key to workplace harmony over the long haul. Crowley and Elster suggest that regular self-checks can help us identify common emotional, mental and physical stressors. Anger, fear, panic and a lack of concentration are a few of the most telling warning signs that all is not well on the job. Some of the more obvious physical indicators are clenched teeth, neck and head pain, and shortness of breath. So what is a troubled worker to do?

Crowley and Elster suggest the four-step plan on the next page to help free ourselves from workplace stressors in every situation, no matter how emotionally charged.

FREEDOM FROM WORKPLACE STRESSORS

- **Step 1** — Unhook physically. Step away from the environment, take a quick walk, or use deep-breathing techniques until an inner calmness returns.
- **Step 2** — Unhook mentally. Separate the emotional from the rational by stepping back and doing some fact gathering.
- **Step 3** — Unhook verbally. Use deliberate, focused speaking to encourage problem solving.
- **Step 4** — Unhook with a business tool. Make full use of company procedures such as written job descriptions, performance standards and reviews.

Fundamentals

By this time you ought to be teachers yourselves, yet here I find you need someone to sit down with you and go over the basics on God again, starting from square one—baby's milk, when you should have been on solid food long ago!
HEBREWS 5:12

*U*pon awakening every morning, we would be wiser, more at-peace women if we were to give our first thoughts to God. Our very best and highest aspirations for today — for every day — should be to know and honor God more fully. But given the intensity with which people, projects and responsibilities pull at us, it is difficult to be single-minded unless we make a deliberate effort to make God our number one priority. We honor God with our best and first thoughts of the day by spending time reading the Bible, meditating on God's promises, making them our very own for the coming hours and the coming decisions. In the process, we change — we are renewed from the inside out. As we put off the harried scattered thinking of the day and put on biblical promises and purposes, our minds are energized and activated. We are ready for making the tough choices, those that will challenge both our heart and our mind. The more we consciously make an internal and eternal investment in God's promises, the more we can be confident in our ability to make decisions that will be both good and worthy.

Rocky Road

Marlene sat on her horse, grappling uneasily with the leather reins in one hand and holding tight to the saddle horn with the other.

"What exactly did the guide say before we mounted?" she asked herself. "Don't rely on the saddle to keep you upright, use your legs, balance your body equally on his back and learn to anticipate your horse's intentions."

Marlene really *did* want to go on this ride with her three closest friends. But as soon as the guide began his spiel on the basic rules of horsemanship, she had felt a tremor of trepidation. Was this a mistake?

Checking herself, Marlene squelched that negative thought. "How hard can it be?" she reasoned. "We'll be riding in a straight line through the mountains with guides at both the head and rear." Still, once the stable hand had helped ease her onto her saddle, she felt stricken.

"I don't know if I can do this," she worried. "Safely, that is. Let's see, I have to make sure the horse knows I'm the boss. I can't let him eat anything once we get on the trail. And the big no-no is allowing him to get too close to the mount in front of us. Or else." Marlene gulped. She certainly did not want to be kicked by an irritated two-thousand-pound beast sporting iron shoes. Before she could change her mind and beg off the four-hour trip, the guide whistled. Her horse seemed to know his business and set off on the dusty path.

Marlene paid attention to her horse's every movement. While the horses in front of her nibbled the leaves from the surrounding trees, Marlene kept her horse on the straight and narrow. When they arrived at a stream, Marlene got her horse through without him stopping for a drink — another small, but satisfying accomplishment. Over, around, up and down the rocky paths they rode until Marlene's knees and backside ached.

Finally, they arrived at the halfway point where a stunning waterfall awaited them. Here the horses could ease their burdens, and Marlene could stretch and walk off her soreness. Taking advantage of the twenty-minute break, she made her way to the bottom of the gorge and perched on a log. She closed her eyes and heard only the cascading water as it rushed downstream. Marlene breathed deeply as the misty air and the scents of summer engulfed her senses.

"How I wish the entire trip could be as carefree as this," she mused. "How I wish life could be like this."

"Listen, just listen," she whispered. "Drink in the wonder of this magical place while you still have the opportunity."

And so she did.

"The poor and homeless are desperate for water,
their tongues parched and no water to be found.
But I'm there to be found, I'm there for them,
and I, God of Israel, will not leave them thirsty."
ISAIAH 41:17- 18

Whether our failure was simple carelessness, the inability to perform up to standard, or the seemingly random strike of circumstances, we need to refuse to let it define us for the rest of our lives. We can let it become a page in our journal but never a reflection in the mirror.
JAMES EMERY WHITE
LIFE-DEFINING MOMENTS

Fundamentals
mind or heart?

> *Those who live from the mind shed few tears.*
> *I wonder if that isn't the real reason they choose to hide there.*
> JOHN ELDREDGE
> *WAKING THE DEAD*

What is the connection between what we *really* want and what we *say* we want? When we think our deepest desires might be considered socially unacceptable (at least in our eyes), we squelch them. Or we deny they exist. Other times, we choose to follow our heart's longings wherever they might lead us and defend our choices after the fact. Both scenarios leave something to be desired. All too often there is a disconnect between our mind (the mental process of making a decision) and our heart (the seat of our emotions, feelings and yearnings).

Whenever we place mind over heart or heart over mind, we risk missing the big picture. Likewise, when either our thoughts or our emotions negate each other, our decision may be lopsided, unbalanced. We need to respect and consider *both* complimentary aspects of our person. We also need the time and space to logically assess each situation, make appropriate responses and allow ourselves to experience the full gamut of emotions — the joy and the pain.

Let's take a closer look at the process of making a decision. Why do we opt for or against a particular course of action? Some would say we act solely for self-preservation, personal advancement, or gratification of our bodily desires. This premise is incomplete at best. Decision-making is much more complex. Our experiences, upbringing, education, beliefs and values help us process even the most basic options almost unconsciously, without a second thought. Still, moving ahead without reflection is as dangerous as refusing to engage our hearts, that is, without any care for the needs of others. This heart disconnect can be just as lethal, maybe more so, as mistaken judgment. When we separate ourselves emotionally from the effects our choices have on others, we can do real harm.

Yes, it takes courage and resilience to choose to engage the heart and the mind. Choosing to enter in emotionally may hurt. Other times it will be a gift. When we engage the whole self — mind and heart, we are more able to make choices that promote balance, goodwill, and other-oriented, consistent results. Joined together, equally regarded, the mind and the heart are an unbeatable combination. We shouldn't neglect either one.

HEAD AND HEART

- Read the chapter of Proverbs that corresponds with the day of the month.
- Read five psalms every day, beginning with the psalm that corresponds with the date. Then read four more psalms in increments of 30. For example, on the second day of the month, read the following psalms: 2, 32, 62, 92 and 122.
- For daily reading and study, choose a good classic devotional such as *My Utmost for His Highest* by Oswald Chambers, .
- For deeper, "meatier" daily prayer, try *The Valley of Vision: A Collection of Puritan Prayers and Devotions* by Arthur G. Bennett.

Fragrance

Mostly what God does is love you. Keep company with him and learn a life of love. Observe how Christ loved us. His love was not cautious but extravagant. He didn't love in order to get something from us but to give everything of himself to us. Love like that.

EPHESIANS 5:2

*T*oday, right now, I decide. At this very moment, I choose to allow every portion of my life, my past history, my current emotional stance and my ever-fluctuating physical health, and my over-thinking mind — especially my mind — to determine the happiness of this day.

As I decide to see my life through a lens of faith and opportunity, I have to consider some weighty matters. My life is not lived in a vacuum. What I choose to do affects everyone around me. The inner attitude of my heart flows through my actions, responses and decisions. And all that affects *you*. That inside-of-me heart intent almost always reveals itself in the look on my face. Even when I try to hide my feelings, others see them and react in kind. I have to ask myself if am I reflecting to others what is most important to me — Jesus' love. His gaze, his hands, his voice. That's the very best contribution I can make. The fragrance of his love is always welcome no matter where my day leads me.

We Christians shy away from the word *happiness*, and yet we can invest in the happiness of those around us by modeling true intimacy with our savior and by reflecting that humble, service-minded love.

Shadow Dance

With great grit and determination, Hilary carefully removed the cumbersome wooden shadow box from the wall. She placed it on her kitchen table, taking pains not to tip out any more of the fragile contents than necessary. She really did hate this household task with a vengeance. But with a large family gathering just around the corner, she decided it was long overdue. Not that she minded a little dust here and there, but when her collection of iron figurines, porcelain flowers, or other such finery started growing beard-like cobwebs, she realized she needed to take matters in hand.

Piece by piece, Hilary removed each item and set it down on a corresponding spot on her oak table. She wanted to make sure she was able to fit everything back in place once she'd washed the frame and dusted the individual pieces. "Not like last time," she frowned, remembering how hard it had been to get everything back into its place.

Smiling, Hilary admitted it took skill to find just the right pint-sized remembrances of family events, trips, vacations and holidays. It wasn't always a matter of grabbing just any old thing to place in her shadowbox. Rather, it involved considerable time and care.

Hilary continued removing, dusting and positioning one article after another, lovingly caressing each one as it evoked a particular memory. "This pale yellow egg marked the fourth year we rented that cottage on the lake. Now, this speckled one represented our first venture into cottaging…a vacation drenched with rain and family discord," she remembered with a sigh

Picking up the tiny conch shell, she held it up to her ear and listened closely, smiling as she could just make out the faint sounds of the ocean. Two high school class rings. Assorted jelly-like animals filled with liquid soap. A rubbery Bullwinkle-shaped eraser from childhood. The metal cross necklace given by a friend after a spiritual retreat. The postage stamps from an overseas friend.

Hilary looked at each treasure and felt so blessed. While not every piece she'd saved represented a perfect memory, each one had something to say about her life. Many spoke of the brightest, most shining moments, but others items, like the speckled egg, reminded her of painful times. Yet, all in all, she believed that looking back without regret helped her keep pace with today's challenges.

Hilary suddenly realized why she put off cleaning this memory keeper. Once she got started, it took her all day! She just couldn't help herself from stopping, smiling and revisiting the times God had given her.

"At that same time, a fine vineyard will appear.
There's something to sing about!
I, GOD, tend it.
I keep it well watered.
I keep careful watch over it
so that no one can damage it."
ISAIAH 27:2-3

It's not your outlook but your "up look" that counts.
GOD'S LITTLE DEVOTIONAL JOURNAL FOR WOMEN

Fragrance

*choosing happiness,
choosing life*

*We cannot choose to be born,
and we cannot opt out of death.
Birth and death are constants for all people.
But we can choose how to live.*
DAVID D. IRELAND
SECRETS OF A SATISFYING LIFE

In his book *Secrets of a Satisfying Life*, David D. Ireland looks closely at statistical evidence about the lifestyle choices of individuals who consider themselves very happy. Bottom line: The happiest people are those who help others. Other researchers have discovered similar characteristics of those who report consistent satisfaction with their lives. One essential characteristic is a healthy perspective: The way life is *seen* and *interpreted* makes all the difference. Another characteristic is the habit of evaluating and reevaluating. This practice helps in responding to both the good and bad that come into every life.

Ireland recommends responding to the following questions when difficulties arise.

- Am I responding impulsively?
- Is this the worst thing that can happen to me?
- What do I want my future to look like?
- How can I establish a strategy for happiness as part of the overall solution?

As Ireland writes, "Bad news cannot be responded to impulsively…and a level-headed response will help maintain a positive state of mind." He also notes that individuals must not make the mistake of equating positive thinking with happiness. Rather, "habits of happy people are deliberate responses that have successfully proven to meet their personal emotional needs."

When we look for a happy person, Ireland believes, we will not find her *searching* for happiness. Instead, the happy individual will be found building, writing, educating, growing. In other words, she will be *making conscious choices* on a moment-by-moment basis to enrich her life and the lives of those around her. Further, Ireland says, "Happiness can and is to be found in the measure of satisfaction one can find in the normal activities of life." Rather than *searching* for the perfect job, mate, house, or vacation, happy people *see* and *focus* on the good amidst life's flaws and shortcomings.

HABITS FOR A HAPPY LIFE

- Recognize and establish a reasonable threshold of satisfaction so that more experiences are deemed positive.
- Embrace a hopeful outlook. As someone once said, "Hopelessness is a coma of the soul."
- Develop a true portrait of who you are and who you are not. Then work to achieve those dreams and goals within this informed framework.
- Balance activity with regular periods of rest.
- Allow sincerity, vulnerability and forgiveness their proper place in all relationships.
- Don't allow pain or past mistakes to paralyze you. Realize the future is a friend.

Regret

So watch your step. Use your head.
Make the most of every chance you get.
EPHESIANS 5:15

*E*ver wonder how the false ideal of being perfect, living a perfect existence, enjoying perfect relationships affects us? True enough, God tells us to do all "as onto the Lord," giving our very best in every situation. But God also understands our weaknesses, our failings and our sin. Rather than allowing past regrets to overshadow tomorrow's promise for health, healing and hope, we must believe our God is able to bring the truest restoration. God desires that we view our regrets accurately, seek forgiveness for wrongdoing, make restitution as we are able, and then move forward.

Catch that? *Move on.* By faith, through God's strength, and with God's grace, we step forward into the future, confident God is able to make all things beautiful in his time. All things.

Sanctuary

With her dog-eared journal in one hand and her other grasping her bike handle, Jill looked up as a shadow passed overhead. Spying the eagle that nested a mere mile from her home, she pedaled along as fast as she dared. She already knew where the two bald eagles had their nest — up, way up, in a tree well over a hundred feet high. She had long wanted to see one of the mature eagles land in their tree top abode, but thus far she had only seen them soaring.

Speeding along the path, Jill ceased her sky gazing and pressed on. Another half-mile down the road and she'd be there. Braking fast, she skidded, stones flew, and she dropped her journal. Looking up, she frowned. "I'm too late. The eagle's already landed. Still," Jill pondered, "if I'm patient enough, I might see him take off again."

Parking her bike off the road, Jill settled down to wait. After seeing no sign of movement from the nest, she turned her attention to her journal. She always took a few minutes each evening to write about the events of her life, but in eleven years of faithful journaling had never once reread her entries. Today she decided to see what she'd considered important enough to write about in her early married and mothering days.

Paging through her journal, Jill noted that she'd been consistent even back then. Almost every day had a minimum of one page full of her scribblings. "This should be interesting," she thought.

Jill opened the book to page one. By page four, she was shaking. "Who was this person? Did I really ever feel this way about my husband? Was I such an irritable mom?" Jill felt scarcely able to continue.

Feeling her stomach twist, Jill closed the journal. Then she experienced a rush of shame and guilt. "I can't believe I wrote all that down in black and white. What if my husband or kids ever got their hands on this? They'd think I didn't love them."

Mortified, Jill wondered if she'd changed much over the years. Certainly she didn't feel or even agree with the journal entries she'd just read. "I do believe I've grown," she considered soberly.

A shadow passed overhead. "The eagle," Jill realized. "He's taken off again looking for more food. What I wouldn't give to have wings to fly up and away.... Then again, even the eagle returns home to roost each day. Maybe what I need most is to go back home and make sure I leave a legacy I'll be proud of."

"I'm absolutely convinced that nothing — nothing living or dead, angelic or demonic, today or tomorrow, high or low, thinkable or unthinkable — absolutely nothing can get between us and God's love because of the way that Jesus our Master has embraced us.
ROMANS 8:38-39

The heft of a pen in my hand with the things of God on my mind has often been good for my soul. Try it for yours.
DONALD S. WHITNEY
SIMPLIFY YOUR SPIRITUAL LIFE

Regret

moving on

> And between the old and new — the "was" and the "not
> yet" — there exists only one thing: a very frightening journey
> called faith. It is stripped of the usual comforts. It comes in
> one color: dark. It offers one amenity: catharsis.
>
> MARGARET BECKER
> *COMING UP FOR AIR*

If we're honest, we'll admit we all long for the bonuses, benefits and blessings that positive change can offer. True enough: The future is expansive, ripe with possibility, and can appear quite friendly on certain days, under specific circumstances. Depending upon our perspective and resiliency of spirit, tomorrow may be viewed as an opportunity full of promise. Or not.

Balance this optimism with the sobering fact that *personal transformation* is a lifelong process, something we believers call progressive sanctification. The passage from who we *are* to who we *can be* never ceases. It is not surprising, then, that most of us wrestle with the personal adversary — formidable foe that it is — of regret. Choruses of "shoulda, woulda, coulda" haunt men and women alike, the young and old and everyone in between. We *all* have said, done, failed to do, or thought something we've ultimately come to regret. We *all* must reckon with our personal mistakes, wrong choices and ill-made decisions. How, then, can we summon up the courage to walk forward?

Paul Tripp, author of *Lost in the Middle*, says, "...the more life you have behind you, the more dreams give way to reflection, and before long you are spending much more time looking back than looking forward. You become a regular spectator on the person that once was. And you don't always like what you see." Ouch. Isn't it a paradox that even at our worst we can be remade for the good? But for this transformation to take place, we must face past regrets with honesty and courage, and be willing to learn from these mistakes. Finally, we must face the future with expectation and hope, forging new habits and making new lifestyle choices day by day and even hour by hour.

When we face our failings, something significant can happen, something quite wonderful, in fact. Tripp shares that, as clarity is realized, "This moment of personal honesty and truth can be crushing and paralyzing, or it can be the beginning of a remarkably new phase of redemptive insight, change and personal celebration."

- Regret is futile, inefficient and unproductive. It offers nothing by way of solution.
- Regret paralyzes. Forward movement can't coexist with fear-bound inactivity.
- Regret cannot make amends. Only pro-active restorative actions can bring healing.
- Regret is shortsighted, fixed on yesterday's failings. It prevents us from seeing the whole picture.
- Regret produces anxiety, fear and dread, short-circuiting both physical and mental health.
- Regret denies the possibility of change and refuses to seek help in order to change.
- Regret is a thief that robs and robs and robs, never to be satisfied.

Contentment

Yes, there's a right time and way for everything,
even though, unfortunately, we miss it for the most part.
ECCLESIASTES 8:6

In the rush-rush of everyday life, do you find yourself frequently anxious embracing a let's-just-get-through-it mentality? So often when life presses in, we daydream about a quieter, more peaceful existence. We fool ourselves into thinking that our current busyness is just temporary. That today's and tomorrow's rush-rush to get things done will pass quietly away into oblivion. But it isn't so. Life is busy. Still, God's word says there is a proper time for everything under the sun. It's absolutely essential to learn how to balance and prioritize.

And yet, the life we live is *now*, and the *process* is the stuff of life. Sure, we'll get to our destinations one way or another, but wouldn't it be lovely to see all of life's seasons and stages fitting in just right with God's plans for us? It *can* be so. We simply need to readjust our lens to see all of life's happenings as part of a much grander scheme. Today we decide what to make of our moments, our hours. We determine what to put our hearts and hands to, and what to let go of as we passionately pursue God and the highest personal plan for us.

Parched

Valerie dashed into the house, dropped her purse and went straight to her answering machine, scribbling notes as she listened to and then deleted messages. Making a beeline for her office, she grabbed the family calendar and went online, hoping to forestall the inevitable gut-wrenching feeling in her middle as she opened her filled inbox.

"More commitments," she despaired. Despite any misgivings about the rapid pace at which their summer schedule was becoming full to overflowing, she dutifully handled her incoming mail, reading, deleting or responding to each message, or filing whatever required more time for a decision.

When she was finished, Valerie decided to tackle the single most disagreeable task she could imagine — an urgent need to appeal to her husband before he arrived home from his business trip. After solo parenting for two straight weeks, she was spent. It wasn't just her spouse's absence that fatigued her. It was also his daily emails, full of plans complicating their already frantic lifestyle.

"When he's home, Tim loves to make the most of his time," Valerie thought. "And when he's due home, I'm ready for a reprieve, not more company. Still, I need to be willing to compromise." Even as she thought this, she felt her conviction waning.

Deciding how to best word her note of desperation to Tim, one that would lay out their burgeoning schedule and persuade him to free up some of their precious family time, Valerie sat with fingers on the keyboard...waiting for some inspiration. Then the doorbell rang. "It's the landscaper," Valerie rejoiced. "I'm saved...at least for a while."

Unlocking the gate, Valerie ushered her garden designer — a favorite senior-citizen friend — into her backyard. As was her habit, Valerie hung around, soaking in tips on the best way to care for her cactus beds and desert-loving flowers.

"Remember," he cautioned her, "these aren't the kind of plants that need lots of water. You're not living in the Midwest anymore. These plants thrive in the hot sun and dry air. Don't fuss. Just be patient, and they'll surprise you with their resilience."

Valerie nodded, suddenly aware of a parallel to her dilemma with her husband. "Maybe I shouldn't be in such a rush to straighten things out with Tim," she thought. "Perhaps it would be better to keep my hands off, exercise a little patience, and wait until he's rested and settled in before I hit him with the wrinkles in his plans."

The right word at the right time
is like a custom-made piece of jewelry.
PROVERBS 25:11

Most of us, perhaps, live in not a terribly evil place in the
moralistic sense of the word. We simply live where busyness,
or apathy, or struggle with circumstances that won't change
occupies most of our energy. And the enemy is perfectly
happy to leave us in such a place practicing our religion.
BRENT CURTIS AND JOHN ELDREDGE
THE SACRED ROMANCE

Contentment

putting things in order

> *One of the greatest life lessons you can ever learn*
> *is to enjoy life through the process of attaining your goals.*
> DAVID D. IRELAND
> *SECRETS OF A SATISFYING LIFE*

On any given day, we can be caught in the act of daydreaming. Not that daydreaming is a bad exercise; sometimes the most winning plans have been hatched during these mental wanderings. But daydreaming can also hinder our forward progress and fill us with disappointment, frustration and impatience. It can even keep us from appreciating the beauty of the present moment.

It's pretty clear that we women experience pressure to succeed. We may fill multiple roles, personal and professional, each vying for our attention. If we're smart, we'll recognize that these responsibilities do not define our life as a whole.

Life can change in an instant and often does, but there is something to be said for viewing life — the few-and-far-between glamorous moments and the more mundane — as *all* worthwhile. Everything we do in the next twenty-four hours prepares us in some measure for tomorrow. Whether we long for greatness in some obscure professional field or simply hanker to excel at gardening matters little. Our focus, our intent, must be on giving our all *today.*

Sadly, we often spend precious time wandering mentally into tomorrow's unknown, feeding our feelings of discontent, feelings that can that override our good judgment. Yes, today's difficulties *do* take a toll. Still, armed with a positive outlook, we can use these hardships as stepping-stones to future success. It's all in the viewpoint and the end goal. Learning to take everything in stride enables us to invest in this day's work while contemplating the future.

David Ireland reminds us that, as we seek to live fully on this given day, "the destination seems nearer and the view *is* more picturesque." It is possible to be totally present in the now and still have a vision for tomorrow. It is!

THE ENEMIES OF CONTENTMENT

- **Exhaustion** — mental, emotional and physical. Take care to daily balance work and rest.
- **Purposelessness.** Dream big, and then make practical plans.
- **Unreasonable expectations.** Be satisfied with doing the best you can.
- **Shortsighted perspectives.** Today's shortfall isn't the last or final word.
- **Selfishness.** Discipline yourself to look beyond your own wants, needs and desires.

Respect

Good Sense will scout ahead for danger,
Insight will keep an eye out for you.
PROVERBS 2:11

Being spared an angry response after having made a terrible mistake. Breathing a sigh of relief when an anticipated rejection never transpires. Experiencing mercy instead of punishment, especially when we know we deserve it. Haven't we all been on the receiving end of one of these blessings?

Admitting our natural tendency to give back what others give us, we probably deserve some rebuke and upbraiding. In our hearts, we all understand this to be true. And yet, we follow Jesus' example most closely when we give others precious gifts of words spoken with respect and dignity, responses laced with mercy, and kindness framed with understanding. People might not expect this kind of response. They might not believe it. They might even scoff at it, and they probably won't thank us for it, but they may wonder why we're offering such gracious words. Beyond the obvious good that good words can do, there's a heaven-sent promise that goes part and parcel with this principle. As we speak discretely and with wisdom, thinking the best, not the worst, we are protected, as it says in God's word, by goodness, mercy and kindness. Who knew that giving someone words of life would, in turn, bring goodness to us?

Mercy Me

Kim spent the later half of the afternoon perched on her window seat looking our over her backyard. Like her mood, the weather was stormy and dark, and the dampness was pervasive. She watched the puddles form as the rain pelted down. If it continued to rain much longer, the stream out back would likely flood her basement again. "It's depressing," Kim pronounced. "All this gloom and doom on my one day off this week."

Tomorrow, Kim realized, she'd be back in the thick of it again. All that office reorganization was wearing thin. She admitted she'd not been too quiet about her dislike of the office overhaul. Even the previous afternoon, during a late lunch, she had joined right in with the others as they had a good ole' time bashing the new office supervisor. Kim laughed when her co-worker John made some off-color remarks about their superior. "It was funny," she defended herself to her conscience later that evening. "It was!"

Still, Kim knew better. Once she'd gotten on the bandwagon a few weeks earlier and had made her feelings known, everyone else assumed she agreed with every petty slight and derogatory comment they uttered. The truth was Kim *did* understand their arguments. She *did* agree that management had instituted some unfair policies But were her snide remarks making the situation any better? No.

Kim realized that she was now siding with the majority of her co-workers in their rising tide of angry recrimination. During one of the more lively debates, her conscience moved her to turn things around by posing some more positive alternatives, including a solution or two, to counter all the negativity. But they laughed at her. They thought she was joking.

"So much for my credibility," Kim agonized. So she kept quiet and tried to play it cool…until yesterday when she had given in yet another time to the negativity that surrounded her. She felt vindicated at the time, but today all she experienced was a wash of shame.

"Lord," Kim prayed, "you're doing a bang up job using the rain to wash all the dirt and sediment away outside my window. Will you do the same inside my heart?"

"But oh! God is in his holy Temple!
Quiet everyone—a holy silence. Listen!"
HABAKKUK 2:20

All my problems become smaller when I confront them. If I touch a thistle with caution, it will prick me, but if I grasp it boldly, its spines crumble into dust.
ANDY ANDREWS
THE TRAVELER'S GIFT

Respect
for others
and for yourself

> *Whatever games are played with us,*
> *we must play no games with ourselves.*
> RALPH WALDO EMERSON

"I won't even dignify that comment with a response." Haven't we all heard someone offer this curt reply? After all, when we feel we've been misjudged, maligned or insulted, it's only natural to offer this type of comeback. But is it effective? Does it promote understanding and reconciliation? Does taking a verbal jab at someone *ever* make sense?

Consider this. Each time we speak or refuse to speak, we're taking a chance. Depending upon our mood, our health and our current emotional state, the person we're addressing is also taking a risk. She doesn't know what we've faced in the previous twenty-four hours. She has no clue how the pressures and frustrations of the day have weighed us down. Add to that volatile mix the speaker's own state of mind. The combination can be lethal.

Whether in the workplace or in the home, we need to find ways to handle life's demands and stresses. Sadly, we can't always see the struggles of the people we encounter. And yet, we *have* to communicate to reach understanding. Opting out of verbal exchanges isn't an alternative. We could hesitate. Or we could charge in with a brutal frontal assault. Let's look at some alternatives.

There's no law that says we have to mirror another's bad behavior. We don't have to play verbal chess games, trying to outwit our opponent. It isn't always "us against them." Often a cranky person is just plain worn out.

There's a better way, and it's right in front of our faces. It's called offering dignity. You know, that inner willingness to extend forgiveness, care and respect — a gift the other may not expect. The bottom line is this: When we treat another person with kindness and dignity, we only enhance our own. Likewise, when we choose to denigrate or devalue another person, we also devalue ourselves.

How much more pleasant life would be if we offered one another basic consideration. Why not make an effort to demonstrate genuine courtesy each and every day beginning this very moment?

DIY DIGNITY

- **D** — **Do** set the tone for a conversation by expressing appreciation and thanks from the outset.
- **I** — **Invite** positive feedback by pairing considerate verbal cues with friendly non-verbal ones.
- **G** — **Graciously** ask for assistance, advice or cooperation.
- **N** — **Never** discuss hot topics if your emotional temperature is rising fast. Wait until tempers cool.
- **I** — **Initiate** an atmosphere of open exchange by listening intently and without interrupting.
- **T** — **Take** the required time to talk. Don't rush through a litany of requests.
- **Y** — **Yield** the day if need be. Brainstorm new ways to speak and be heard on another day.

Fidelity

Help your servant — I'm depending on you!
You're my God; have mercy on me.
I count on you from morning to night.
PSALM 86:2

an't be too careful, right? Wrong. God calls us to be courageous in facing down our fears and worries. God doesn't want us wasting our time worrying, fretting, in hand-wringing immobility. Rather, God wants us to know the divine love so well, trust the divine spirit so implicitly, that we never, ever shudder or quake when faced with the known or unknown challenges of daily life. Instead, God encourages us — admonishes us — to believe, to trust, to step out and make our move, to press ahead instead of pulling back. Indeed, we are called to live conscientious and careful lives. God promises to guard us and guide our ways as we seek him through prayer and diligent study of the Bible.

This careful approach means that we refuse to live in fear, always pausing to look over our shoulders, wondering when catastrophe will hit. Rather, we move into our days with the bold assurance given by God's Spirit and with humility flowing from our utter dependence upon Christ to see us through. Think of it as *bold humility*. Now that's something that will surely serve us well for care-full living!

Heart Tug

Emma opened the letter and felt a rush of relief. At last she knew she'd have enough money for food, rent and gas for the next three months. After resigning from her position at the bank and heading back to school full-time, she needed a full-time, good-paying summer job to help offset her living expenses. "If I work full-time in the summer," she considered, "then I'll only need a weekend job to make ends meet during the school year."

As Emma continued reading, she reacted with a sudden intake of breath. "No way!" she cried. "They never told me at the agency that I'd be assigned to work on the island. I can't possibly take the ferry over twice a day. I just can't."

Repressing a shudder, Emma wanted to cry. "There it goes, my perfect job. Now what will I do?" She tried to calm herself down. "Think," she told herself. "There's no other job where I'll earn as much. Besides I wanted employment in a private home. It would be good experience to work as a nurse's aide before getting my RN degree."

"But Lord," Emma continued, "*can* I do it? You know my secret fear of water. You were there when I almost drowned. It was a close shave. If my brother hadn't been looking for me, it would have been too late. I'm still deathly afraid of water."

Closing her eyes and emitting a deep sigh, Emma recognized that gentle, almost unrecognizable tug within her heart. "Okay, what better time to overcome my fear of water than now, right?"

Day by day, Emma crossed out the dates on her calendar. Before long she'd be compelled to board the town's ferry twice a day. Anxious and afraid, she couldn't take the pressure any longer. She grabbed her purse and car keys and resolutely drove down to the docks. With determination, she purchased a round trip ticket and boarded the ferry.

Making her way to the top level, as far from the water below as possible, Emma sat down and prayed. "Lord, I need your peace, and I need it now. Help me face down this childhood fear. I have allowed it to paralyze me for far too long. Give me the strength to see this journey through because I'm confident that you have wonderful things in store for me on the other side. Amen."

I want each of you to take plenty of time to think it over, and make up your own mind what you will give. That will protect you against sob stories and arm-twisting. God loves it when the giver delights in the giving.
2 CORINTHIANS 9:7

Nowhere in Scripture is self-denial seen as an end in itself, but always a means to a greater end. For the believer, that greater end is not becoming a dour, rigidly committed disciple of Christ. It's becoming a God-satiated, Christ intoxicated, Spirit-empowered worshiper and servant of the Most High God.
DWIGHT EDWARDS
RELEASING THE RIVERS WITHIN

Fidelity

careful choices

*Some persons do first, think afterward,
and then repent forever.*

Thomas Secker

How would you describe yourself? Are you a careful person, thoughtfully weighing decisions and potential repercussions before acting? Or would you consider yourself a free-flying-live-by-the-moment carefree — careless — type? There is no right or wrong answer here. It's simply a matter of degree. Certainly, the woman who notices things — you know, is *in tune* with the feelings, inclinations, likes and dislikes of those around her — will act in accordance with what she observes. If she's careful, that is. What could be more boorish, that is, careless, than a person who consciously offends another?

On the flip side, some of us appear to live in a world of our own making. We do what we please whenever, wherever and to whomever we choose. We've all been victims of someone's careless, self-serving decision, and we recognize the harm it does. So does everyone else — except perhaps the offender.

But is there such a thing as living too carefully? Indeed, there is. Too much thinking — over-thinking — leads to fearful indecision, inaction and lack of involvement. To strike a balance between the two extremes, might we not aim for some middle ground? Could we live with the awareness that every choice made *in favor* of something is also a choice *against* something else? Given only so much time, energy and resources, we each need to decide how to make careful choices for living, working and playing.

This leads to a logical conclusion: Every decision we make today will support or strengthen the people in our lives or it will tear them down. Which will it be? If we're committed to living carefully, we will experience strong relationships, better physical health, sounder finances, and overall increased bountiful living. Final word: Take good care. It's the recipe for a full and fruitful life.

How to Spot a Care-full Person

- Engages an "antenna of awareness," that is, makes an effort to be sensitive to those around her.
- Makes only those promises she can keep and then makes good on every one.
- Anticipates the needs of others and looks out for ways to meet those requirements.
- Recognizes that relationships on every level are privileges to be treated with respect.
- Takes a big-picture view of life even when circumstances are grim.
- Enjoys the journey and, by example, invites others to do the same.

Waiting

Don't quit in hard times;
pray all the harder.
ROMANS 12:12

Does anyone really enjoy waiting? The very word can have negative undertones. Rarely do we hear or meet a person who welcomes the wait. True enough, waiting can feel like wasted time, misspent hours, lost time, forfeited opportunity to *do* something — anything. But waiting can also help us change on the inside where no one else can see. That is, as we learn to slow our pace, we can change for the better. There's good reason why Alexander Pope is still quoted hundreds of years after he wrote "fools rush in" — in the *rushing* we often make foolish and foolhardy mistakes, errors that could be avoided or minimized if we sit still long enough and think hard enough. If only we could wait. And wait well.

Weathering

Jackie peered outside at the pouring rain and realized she'd left her mother's cactus out on the deck. She hunted around for an umbrella, but after looking high and low, gave up. "Sorry, cactus man," she lamented. "I guess you're going to have to weather this downpour without my help."

The sky continued to empty its contents for hours on end while Jackie worked around the house getting everything in order before her children returned from their first day of school. What a day it had been already! Jackie had been up and about since 5:30 a.m. making scrambled eggs and toast, packing lunches, and generally overseeing everyone's departure.

Unlike other first-day-of-school mornings, she had been nervous. Her youngest son Blake was starting his first day of high school, and Jackie was strung higher than a kite. Even though he had fared well academically in past years, she felt for him. He wasn't following in his older brothers' footsteps. Rather, in just about every possible way, Blake had taken his own road. Quiet and introspective, he seemed more than content to be alone. He didn't seek out other boys his age or have any desire for a little companionship. This preyed on Jackie's mind constantly, and she wondered what she could do to encourage him to be more sociable. So far, nothing had been effective.

Jackie also fretted that, because Brett was different, the other kids would give him grief. So far that hadn't happened. So why worry? She admitted the real issue was her own fear of losing control over her children's lives. She didn't want them — or in this case, Blake — to travel down a road where she couldn't direct from the sidelines. Blake's situation wasn't ideal, but lacking any immediate solution, she realized her only way to support him was to pray. So pray she did. And wait. Praying and waiting were to become her daily practice.

As Jackie continued to complete her to-do list, the rain stopped, the clouds finally parted, and the sun even peeked out. When she took her basement rugs outside for a good shaking, she noticed how well her mother's cactus was doing. "I can't believe it," she exclaimed. "With all the extra rain we've had and my forgetting to bring you inside, you're still thriving! Despite all the unfavorable conditions!"

Jackie was secretly encouraged by the tenaciousness of this prickly plant. Inspecting it yet more closely, she felt better about Blake's situation too. "Circumstances may be of my control," she thought, "but difficulties can become the impetus for productive growth. I might have to watch and wait for years to actually see progress and growth with my physical eyes, but there's nothing wrong with using my spiritual eyes until that day arrives."

If you fall to pieces in a crisis,
there wasn't much to you in the first place.
PROVERBS 24:10

Don't bother to give God instructions;
just report for duty.
GOD'S LITTLE DEVOTIONAL JOURNAL FOR WOMEN

Waiting

attitude makeover

> *How do we get to the morning,*
> *to the sunshine, to the joy?*
> *There is only one way.*
> *By waiting for it.*
> KEN GIRE

Remember that old saying, "I scream, you scream, we all scream for ice cream"? Well, in today's world ice cream isn't what's causing most folk to run around screaming in silent frustration. It's *waiting.* We're a sorry bunch of wait-ers, aren't we? Our entire nation wants — no, demands — that needs be met immediately. Whether what we want is small or large, it matters not. Americans young and old are continually being fed the lie that if we desire something, it is within our power and rights to obtain it — now! No delay required.

Too bad real life begs to disagree. And disagree it does. Consider all our experiences of waiting. We wait to get better after feeling ill. We wait for someone to reply to an urgent request. We wait for doctors, dentists, hair stylists, spouses, children. We wait in lines. We wait for our turn. We wait to be heard. We wait to be found or found out. We wait for a better job. We wait to complete our education. We wait for repair technicians, parts, labor, bills. We wait to hear the weather, the sports news, evening news, bad news, good news, any news at all. Let's face it, for a huge portion of our lives we must wait.

Since waiting is life and life is waiting, why not learn to wait the best way we can? Let's look at our assumptions and learn to view wait time as an opportune time to develop quietude, listen better, see more clearly, contemplate tough decisions, reflect, and be thankful. We can do this. We *can*. If we choose to channel all that anxiety-ridden energy in new and positive directions, our waiting will be transformed, and we'll be changed. And, as we accept waiting as a necessary ally rather than a mortal adversary, everything about us will change too. We'll find more time for what's important, for appreciating the subtle beauty of daily life, and for resting contentedly wherever we find ourselves. We can take comfort in that fact that time is fluid, moving, never stagnant. No matter how long or painful the wait, the waiting won't last forever. History proves this. We should know by now that hope comes to those who wait.

Author Ken Gire writes, "We can't hurry the dawn, no matter how anxiously we pace the floor or how impatiently we watch the clock. And so the question is not do we wait or not wait, because waiting is all we can do. The question is, how will we wait? Will we wait well...or will we wait poorly?"

- **W — Warm up** to the concept of waiting well. Think back to all the times you rushed ahead, emotionally propelled, rather than taking one thoughtful step at a time. How often did you ever really benefit from rushing ahead? Moreover, how frequently did rushing cause undue pain for you or someone else?

- **A — Accept** waiting as an integral part of life. Despite our hurry-hurry mentality, waiting can do us good when we accept it, make peace with it, and quietly allow it to do its inner work in our hearts and minds.

- **I — Instill** periods of waiting into your hours and days. Set aside precious minutes to simply be still. See how these moments of inactivity help you to re-interpret what's really important. We learn to see better and live better by stepping back, stepping out of the fray, and taking responsibility for the time allotted us.

- **T — Talk back** to yourself during those stretches when waiting feels unbearable. Don't just listen to negative self-condemning mind chatter. Speak against it with the truth found in God's promises of his faithfulness, his unchangeableness, his constancy, even in unnerving circumstances.

Fearlessness

"Be strong. Take courage. Don't be intimidated. Don't give them a second thought because GOD, your God, is striding ahead of you. He's right there with you. He won't let you down; he won't leave you."

DEUTERONOMY 31:6

*W*hen our look is upward, our outlook and our outcomes are unlimited. Only God knows what our hours, days and years will bring. Everything in life is constantly shifting. Nothing, save God and the Bible, is unchanging. We may stay up nights trying to plan, plot and persuade ourselves that we have our lives under control, but in truth, we are not in control of anything. Instead of wasting our precious stores of energy and time, we must train ourselves to "first-thing" cry out to God and believe he will answer. This simple act of faith, which so delights our God, draws us into close peaceful company with Jesus.

We can and should lay our burdens at the foot of the cross, trusting God to give us everything we require to meet the challenges of the day. It is only in Christ that we truly discover courage, peace and the ability to live with credibility and integrity. People notice when we Christ-followers make small, but powerful choices to serve and give, to live quietly and faithfully. May we all seek to mirror Jesus in how we think, act and believe.

Act of Faith

With an air of decisiveness, Ilene marched out to her flower border and started plucking off the deadened remains of the lavender- and fuchsia-colored petunias.

As a novice gardener, she had always approached her beloved flowers with trepidation. She worried that her inexperience would either kill her plants or stunt their growth. So far, she'd been successful with her annuals. Not a one had perished despite this year's long drought. True enough, she spent every evening watering her decorative border. Not to mention the fertilizer she dutifully applied each week as an added insurance that each little sprout would blossom and bloom in hearty fashion. And they had.

Until recently, no one had told Ilene about the practice of deadheading. She didn't want to snip off *any* portion of her flowering plants, be they the now-shriveled leftovers of once beautiful blossoms or not. Still, she listened to the gardening experts and gallantly proceeded to snap and snip her way through the plants along the fence line.

Once she had deadheaded the entire border, she studied the plants. "I hope I did the right thing," she muttered doubtfully.

A few mornings later, Ilene made her cursory round through her yard on her way to fetch the early paper. On her way back to the house, she stopped. She couldn't believe her eyes! Already, tiny buds were popping up from the stems where the previous flowers had grown. Delighted and a bit amazed, she went from plant to plant, examining each one. "I never would have believed it," Ilene admitted. "I thought surely I was killing them."

Within a week, Ilene was again enjoying the quiet beauty of her flowers. As she sat on her side porch admiring the vibrant colors and design of her border, she recognized that nature parallels our spiritual lives.

"How often," she wondered, "has God deadheaded some sinful habit or harmful trait in my own life only to bring forth something truer — something beautiful and pure? I can't begin to count."

"Pearl necklaces and ruby bracelets — why bother?
None of this is even a down payment on Wisdom!"
Job 28:18b

Every person I've ever known who really had something to give has been burst open by the explosive force of God's soul-transforming lessons. Each has been willing to be vulnerable to the truth about themselves, to admit selfishness and behavior patterns that are maddening to other people and destructive to their own souls.
Luci Swindoll
I Married Adventure

Fearlessness

honesty and credibility

Are you a credible person? Do you run a credible business? Given the opportunity, are people eager to place their trust in you? Just how good is your word? Are you comfortable with these questions or are you cringing at some painful missteps you've made in the past, mistakes you really should have remedied?

A credible person can be defined as an expert, someone qualified through experience, intelligence or skill. Of course, we may be adept in some areas and lacking in others. As someone once said, "Credibility is also context-dependent." Does this mean our skill level determines our character and reputation? Yes, no and sometimes. We all know folks who are experts in business but routinely struggle in social situations. Others find it easy to meet and greet family, friends and strangers, but struggle with consistency in school or at work. Depending on the situation, our credibility will either shine brilliantly or flicker to a dim, almost nonexistent flame.

So what's the key to living an all-around credible life? Attitude plus action. Teachability plus humility. A willingness to admit error and make amends.

In today's world complaints about dishonesty are rampant. Wherever dishonesty comes to light — in the business sector, on the golf course, among friends, or in church, we resent its presence and long for the simple honest truth. Certainly, the truth can sting at first, but we instinctively hunger for it, for something and someone we can trust, someone we can depend on in any need, large or small.

Let's be honest here. We've all blown it — every day, perhaps even every hour. Do we give up with despair and regret? With hand wringing and emotional paralysis? Never! We'll always have tomorrow — a new day to start again, to right a wrong, to re-establish credibility and restore relationships by choosing a different course. Certainly, it may be difficult to backpedal or to set off on a different path, but sometimes going back is the only way to make progress. Orlando A. Battista, a renowned chemist, once wrote: "An error doesn't become a mistake until you refuse to correct it." Good words, timely advice and credible counsel for all.

Cause-and-Effect Credibility

- Be a cause-and-effect thinker. Train yourself to think beyond any decisions made today by contemplating what you will set in motion with each yes and no.
- Be a cause-and-effect doer. Remind yourself that God frequently expects us to step out and take action even if we feel we're not ready. Emotional confirmation may come much later.
- Be a cause-and-effect believer. Meditate upon biblical promises every day, make them your own, use them as guidelines for godly living, and count on them to provide inner-strength to face life today and every day forward.

Right

"This is God's work;
we rub our eyes —
we can hardly believe it!"
MARK 12:11

These days, doing what's right can look different to everyone. From the outside, we can appear to be perfect, to be shining examples of righteous living. On the inside, the side no one sees, we know better. Only we understand what it can cost to create and maintain such an image. It might mean ruling the home with little love, with military-like order. Or it might mean cushy emotions and fun, fun, fun while the family sinks under an invisible weight of addiction, debt and slavery to the opinion of others. In any case, we have to decide what matters and what doesn't. Simply put, we have to decide to whom we will listen and what we deem most important.

As we turn to God's word, we read over and over again about God's value system: People matter most. We need to see past today's stuff — material goods and everything visual — and ask God for spiritual eyes that really see what's happening in lives of others. This is the only way we can make a difference, to do good. We actually can inhibit our spiritual growth and hold back the growth of those we love by *not* doing what's right, even when doing what's right seems like the harder road to travel. Doing what's right can be messy, complicated. There aren't many feel-goods moments on this path. Often the consolation of doing right becomes apparent only in retrospect. That's when we see the wisdom of living by faith rather than sight.

On the Trail

Margaret stooped to tie her worn tennis shoes — her walking-away-from-life's-pressures shoes, the ones that had taken her more miles around her property than she'd traveled outside of her small county. Then she grabbed a quick sip of water from the faucet, took her vitamins and headed outside.

That morning Margaret had toiled around the garden, weeding, trimming and just plain tidying up the exterior of the family farm. Tidying up was certainly the most difficult chore. With three youngish children, a husband who loved collecting, and a bevy of dogs and cats, she sometimes lamented that their yard looked as if it was inhabited by vagabonds. Having the property littered with various plastic toys didn't bother the rest of the family, but it sure bothered Margaret. She worked hard to keep the inside of their home in order. "Why can't they cooperate by cleaning up the outside each evening after dinner?" Margaret sighed as she surveyed the section of the yard where her husband kept his "playthings."

She shook her head in despair. "*That's* why," she thought ruefully, "Everything from old spare engine parts to somebody's friend's cousin's used farm equipment has found it's resting place in *my* barn and all around it."

"Like father, like children," she thought. "Why fight what I can't control?"

With that parting sentiment, Margaret left the children with their father, left the dogs in their kennel, left the cats to their own mischief, and took off down the road.

Margaret knew no better tonic for a stressful day than a good walk after finishing her evening chores. It was the hour of the day she relished more than any other. True, the road she walked was dusty, and she had to be careful to avoid the potholes, but she loved nothing better than to hear the gentle swishing of the corn on either side of her or, in another season, the gentle rhythm of the winter wheat blowing back and forth in the wind. It was comforting somehow to be in the midst of such bounty, such beauty, and realize she had no control over what surrounded her.

As she exercised her body, Margaret felt her mind slowly unclutter and her emotions unwind. She even regained some perspective. The longer she spent on the trail, the more she found she was able to accept the challenges of family life.

*"If you're honest in small things,
you'll be honest in big things;
If you're a crook in small things,
you'll be a crook in big things."*
LUKE 16:10

*Be willing to swap a temporary inconvenience
for a permanent improvement.*
H. JACKSON BROWN, JR., AND ROSEMARY C. BROWN
LIFE'S LITTLE INSTRUCTIONS FROM THE BIBLE

Right

the great consolation

> *In many ways, sin is the punishment for sin. The more I choose against God's design and give in to my sinful desires, the more I suffer even if I never get caught, even if no one else knows.*
>
> PHILIP YANCEY

How much would you pay for a clear conscience? To sleep soundly at night? To enjoy a guilt-free existence? To bask in a conflict-free zone with co-workers, family, friends and neighbors alike? Have you ever considered how much value we place on treating one another with courtesy, respect and selflessness?

It's a high stakes gamble these days just locating individuals willing to live sacrificially *in theory* let alone having to actually *make good* on any spoken ideals. In these cynical times, we often wonder if promises will be kept, if a word and a handshake hold any weight. We wonder if society values moral absolutes of any kind. Some even say a definitive sense of right and wrong is outdated, out of touch, passé and better left unsaid. I cannot agree. Since when does doing the right thing ever go out of style? People still need a word of encouragement; surely that's a good thing. People still need a helping hand when they're down; surely that's the right thing to do. People still get sick, some die, while their families grieve; surely, offering comfort is the right thing.

No matter what we say and no matter what society tells us, God has given us a barometer — our conscience — for gauging what's right and wrong. When we make choices that go against this internal warning system, we experience the sting of conscience, we feel guilty, our sleep is disrupted.

So why do we fight it? Wouldn't it be better to do what's right instead of taking the easy route, that is, the wrong route? Think about it, if we're going to experience some type of internal upset in response to our attitudes and actions, wouldn't it be prudent to decide to act rightly toward others from the get-go? We can't lose when we do right. We not only benefit an individual; our actions ripple out to society in general. Changing our world by single acts of kindness. Who knew?

Face it: Whether we like it or not, we reap what we sow. Even when no one else knows what we've done or left undone, *we* know. Wonder when we'll get it right?

RIGHTING THAT WRONG.

- Yesterday isn't over. Unless you've learned some valuable lesson from past mistakes, expect to stay trapped in the same place until you evaluate what didn't work, make a different plan, and change direction.
- Today isn't the last word. Until you lay your head on the pillow for the night, no matter what happened during the past 24 hours, there's always hope for change. It begins with your attitude and responses to the people and circumstances you are facing.
- Tomorrow isn't written yet. Don't anticipate more of the same. Instead, look forward to better.

In the coming days and weeks, you'll be wiser, more astute, more seasoned to handle life and its complexities with faith-fired finesse and grace.

Faithfulness

The Master never lets us down.
He'll stick by you and protect you from evil.
2 THESSALONIANS 3:3

Feelings and emotions...those all-powerful stores of energy we women seem to fight with, against and for our entire lives. Love 'em or hate 'em, we're stuck with them. The rise and fall of these passions can bring us great joy or deep sorrow depending our physical and spiritual well-being. Are we healthy, in the midst of hormonal fluctuations? Have we slept well? Are we trying to live on our own, independent of Christ? Are we trying to get by without his grace and strength? If we feel off-kilter, it could be an early warning sign placed there by our faithful God to draw us back to a place where we and our emotions can be safe 24/7. It doesn't matter if we're feeling up or down. *All* of us need God's continual support. As we lean into Jesus and find renewed strength, we are equipped with the confidence and strength to comfort to those. Blessed be God who comforts us in our time of need so that we in turn can comfort others.

Nocturnal Notions

Punching her pillow into a more comfortable shape, Martha turned on her right side, then rolled back to her left, and a few minutes later lay flat on her back staring at the ceiling. "Since I can't get any rest," she thought, "I might as well get some work done."

Bone tired, Martha grabbed her terry robe and cinched it around her waist. She quietly gathered a couple of books. Very carefully, very quietly, she left the bedroom where her husband's light snores made her glance back at him in frustration.

"It was *your snoring* that woke me and kept me awake," Martha mouthed silently. "Do you realize that?"

Entering their all-seasons porch, she flipped on the light, sat down heavily and made herself comfortable. Looking down at the book she held in her hands, Martha sighed. "What an unlikely chore to be tackling before dawn."

Thumbing through the pages of data made Martha want to cry. "All these numbers, and I can't focus on a one," she lamented. "I need sleep, more of it, more often. I feel depressed, exhausted and out of sorts. How many times in the past several months have I resorted to angry tears as my only release from this exhausting no-win situation?"

"If only Tom would get some help," she went on, " I might not find myself living on the short-end of sleep all the time. *I'm* the one who's constantly and abruptly woken up every night with his snoring. All this dry air isn't helping matters either. How many mornings has Tom gotten up with a dry, irritated throat? I tell him it's all that open-mouth breathing he does! Such a small thing has become a huge issue."

Setting her work aside, Martha's eyes glazed over as she watched the faintest glimmer of light appear over the red rocks in her line of vision. "Sun's coming up," Martha realized. Something inside her urged her, "Turn off the light."

Flicking the switch, Martha turned back to face the slowly-emerging kaleidoscope of colors — a veritable rainbow spreading across the sky in awe-inspiring beauty. With quiet reverence, she studied the contrast of shapes and colors. With increasing awareness and gratefulness for having witnessed this wonder of nature, her eyes filled with tears — not from sorrow or from lack of sleep, but from somewhere deep within her soul. It was her heart's way of thanking God.

"When my life was slipping away,
I remembered GOD,
And my prayer got through to you,
made it all the way to your Holy Temple."
JONAH 2:7

Forgive me if this sounds too simplistic, but the only thing
worth doing is usually the last thing we try doing — turning
it over to God, the Specialist, who has never yet been handed
an impossibility He couldn't handle. Grab that problem by
the throat and thrust it skyward!
CHARLES R. SWINDOLL
STRENGTHENING YOUR GRIP

Faithfulness

helping the depressed

Experts consult; then move on.
Friends and family keep at it.
EDWARD T. WELCH
DEPRESSION: A STUBBORN DARKNESS

Much has been written on the topic of depression, but many of the articles on this issue raise more questions than they answer. While not everyone would agree on the causes of depression or even how much of the experience is physically or emotionally driven, several aspects of this condition are pretty clear: Depressed persons aren't the same as they once were and frequently push away those closest to them when the need for support is greatest. This paradox can be particularly frustrating to loved ones and friends.

The depressed man or woman may not exhibit enthusiasm about anything. What once drove and inspired now lays dormant and discarded. The give and take of relationships can now be overwhelmingly one-sided. Edward Welch, author of *Depression: A Stubborn Darkness*, observes that "...we all shift back and forth between our roles as physician and patient," but that this dynamic is absent when caring people continue to give without getting anything in return from the depressed person. It takes perseverance and persistence to carry on despite repeated rejection by a depressed friend.

Welch cautions that those who try to support and encourage a depressed loved one may experience resistance. It will be hard at times to continue pursuing a loving relationship. "Sometimes," he writes, "you will grow weary in loving. We all do. You will genuinely love, but it will seem fruitless or irrelevant. It won't seem to matter to the depressed person. But know this: *Your love makes a difference.* That doesn't mean one concerted push to love will snap anyone out of depression. By itself, your love will not change anyone."

For a depressed person, time can stand still, but for those observing an emotionally distraught friend, time doesn't pass quickly enough. Family and friends can become impatient for their loved one to move beyond this "phase," for life to get back to normal.

Welch encourages continued effort, believing, "…depressed people, like all of us, are aware of kindness and love that is willing to sacrifice. Love always leaves its mark."

Dr. Welch's Suggestions
for a Helping a Depressed Love One

- Encourage daily structure with regular times for eating, exercising, sleeping.
- Set up a simple schedule to accomplish one new specific task each day.
- Offer accountability. Check in daily with the depressed person.
- Learn to discern the appropriate moments to interrupt faulty speech or thinking patterns and speak the truth.
- Reassure your suffering friend that you are in it for the duration.

Mercy

"Don't lose your grip on Love and Loyalty.
Tie them around your neck;
carve their initials on your heart.
Earn a reputation for living well
in God's eyes and the eyes of the people."
PROVERBS 3:3-4

Circumstances may well appear, well, circumstantial, and yet we may decide to become judge and jury in one fell swoop. We all can remember those painful moments when we were so sure we understood a situation and called it like we saw it, only to discover we didn't have all the facts. Red-faced and ashamed, we had to go back and ask forgiveness.

God's word tells us that mercy triumphs over judgment. Enough said. But if we aren't convinced of this truth and how it protects us and those we might feel tempted to accuse, consider how mercy and truth, when closely knitted to our hearts and souls, will bring favor from God and others. It is a very good thing to be on the receiving end of someone's mercy. We should take good care to remember this experience of mercy the next time we are challenged to decide between extending mercy or condemning.

Tunnel Vision

It was just before lunch when Kelsey returned to their rented beach house to prepare a light snack. Brushing off the grit from her sandals, she took a moment to shake her towel and lay it over the railing before rinsing off and entering the house.

Once inside, she went right to her task, removing fruit from the refrigerator and from the glass bowl which held her arrangement of colorful and unusual fruit. Just eyeing the fresh fruit made her mouth water. At home up north, it was far too early to enjoy the flavor of homegrown strawberries or the delicious first bite of a peach from their own orchard. Wasn't this one of the perks of a late-winter trip south? A chance to relish summer's goodness along with the warmer weather and longer sun-glazed days? A far cry from their frostbitten winter wonderland back home.

Kelsey had hoped that getting away would help ease the pain connected with so many transitions in their lifelong church. Chopping and cutting, she considered how heavy her heart had been these past months. So many reforms, so many families coming and going. It truly grieved her. Kelsey, never one for much change, felt this sudden unsettling transformation was taking its toll on her. Never one to sit back idly and watch life unfold, she longed to do something — anything — to help heal the hurt caused by current climate of unrest. But what? She wasn't in any position to force certain agendas or change people's hearts. No, she reconciled herself to staying busy with her own ministries and offering up prayers on behalf of her congregation.

Still, Kelsey was weary. Some days she even contemplated leaving the church for greener pastures. She pondered that tempting thought as she absentmindedly took a bite of kiwi. "Eeow! How awful!" she grimaced. "I should have listened to what the green grocer told me. He was right. They're not yet fit for consumption."

Shaking her head in dismay, Kelsey painstakingly started removing every slice of kiwi. As she did so, she realized the similarity between her recent attitude toward her ailing church and this single specimen of fruit. Her attitude, the unripe fruit — both could very well spoil the whole.

"Aha," she exclaimed, "Slow learner that I am, I see now that I need to let go and allow God to work things out in *his* time and according to *his* will."

"God's your Guardian,
 right at your side to protect you —
Shielding you from sunstroke,
 sheltering you from moonstroke.
God guards you from every evil,
 he guards your very life.
He guards you when you leave and when you return,
 he guards you now, he guards you always."

PSALM 121:5-8

We are created for community, fashioned for fellowship, and formed for a family, and none of us can fulfill God's purposes by ourselves.

RICK WARREN
THE PURPOSE DRIVEN LIFE

Mercy

giving people the benefit of doubt

> *To be trusted is a greater compliment*
> *than to be loved.*
> GEORGE MACDONALD
> *THE MARQUIS OF LOSSIE*

Making mistakes is part of being human. Every day — more accurately, every hour — we err in areas of judgment, memory, precision or skill. We forget to read an entire report, overlook a deadline, or rush to the next task without first checking our calendars. While we share this tendency to make mistakes, we may not handle our mistakes in the same ways. Likewise, we may respond in different ways to the transgressions of others. In the heat of the moment, do we write people off, cut them from our life? Or do we look for some way to salvage the situation and offer a lifeline to the offender?

Intentionally or not, we often turn mistakes or problems into tangled emotional and spiritual webs. In every situation, we need to decide whether or not to offer someone the benefit of the doubt, to offer forgiveness, or to act as judge and jury.

At times our response to someone who has made a mistake or harmed us depends on the nature of the transgressor, but our disposition can also be a factor in whether or not we offer compassion or grace. Did we enjoy a good breakfast? Have that second cup of coffee? Was the ride to work uneventful? Did our inbox contain the messages we anticipated? Or none of the above? Seems petty, doesn't it? We're so good at blaming and criticizing. It's all too easy to compound one mistake by punishing someone simply to make a point. It just comes so naturally. However, people generally feel bad enough. Dredging up an another's shortcomings does nothing to solve the problem.

Try extending the benefit of doubt instead of believing the worst about another person. It doesn't matter much what they did or didn't do. See how that person responds when you extend trust. Invite the person to right the wrong and communicate your expectation of better results in the future.

Aren't we all too aware of our own shortcomings? Sometimes we're on the edge and all too ready to do battle. Many times we have a me-against-the-world mentality. When someone offers us pardon, grace, a gesture of confidence in our ability to do better, and trust — especially when we might not deserve it, we receive a graced incentive to *do* better, to *be* better. It's a win-win situation for individuals, families, communities and even for businesses.

- M — Our own **mistakes** place us at the mercy of others. Ask yourself how you would like your next misstep to be greeted: with mercy or judgment?
- E — **Every** one of us can say or do something to injure another. What really matters is our heart-intent. Sometimes, though, we just make mistakes by omission or forgetfulness.
- R — We need to **respect** the rights of others to live differently or have opinions that do not match our own. Listening is the best way to gain understanding and build bridges .
- C — We can **cancel out** someone's offense by refusing to dwell on it. When an emotionally charged memory rears its ugly head, we can do an about-face and focus on a positive thought instead.
- Y — We need to **yield** to God's sovereign orchestration of difficult circumstances and resolve to go directly to God for the grace to be both merciful and truthful.

Fulfillment

He does what's best for those who fear him —
hears them call out, and saves them.
PSALM 145:19

*P*erhaps one of the most damaging disservices we believers can inflict upon one another is to promote the non-biblical notion that the only ones who are doing God's bidding are the ones who serve God in full-time church or mission work. Nothing in scripture supports this premise. Rather, God wants *all* of us to be his representatives, servants and workers no matter where God places us. To imply that doctors, lawyers, teachers, stay-at-home moms, farmers and computer technicians aren't fulfilling a specific purpose on earth because they labor outside of an official church setting is a tragedy. How can we miss the mark if we're using our skills and gifts to the best of our ability in our daily lives? God blesses us — every woman and man — as we prayerfully seek guidance, as we put all of our gifts to use for him. What a testimony to our awesome God who delights in watching us shine, reflecting back honor to where it belongs!

In Order

Meg donned her canvas gloves and pith helmet with the protective mesh screening that completely covered her face and neck. She made sure she had on long pants and a long-sleeved shirt. No use inviting a wayward bee to sting her.

Meg sometimes wondered why she went to all this trouble to maintain her hives of honeybees. But every time she harvested the waxy honeycomb and watched the sticky sweet nectar ooze out from the sides, she could almost taste the subtle sweetness of the bees' handiwork. And work it was! Meg marveled at how diligently bees labored at their particular tasks. Like a well-trained worker in a perfectly run factory, each bee knew its job instinctively. Plain and simple. "Which is why my guests and I can reap the benefits of their labor," Meg thought appreciatively. "How I wish I was as certain that my own miniscule vocational contribution made a difference."

With no immediate family to speak of, Meg was a single woman on her own, an entrepreneur running her own bed and breakfast. Lately she had wondered if she had any effect on the world around her. True enough, her business was successful, and she energetically met the needs of her guests. Still, she nursed recurring doubts that she might have missed her true calling some years before when she had dreamed of becoming a nurse and traveling overseas to work as a missionary. Like so many others, Meg had believed that being a truly devout Christian meant living among the destitute. Even though she realized her former notions had been naïve and immature, this as still a sore subject for her.

Shaking herself free of her dark thoughts, Meg turned her attention to the task at hand. Opening the lower tray of the hive, she reached inside to retrieve a honeycomb full of delectable sweetness. "Won't my guests just love dribbling this over their muffins in the morning!" she anticipated happily. "Maybe I'll even join them this time and sneak in a short lesson on honeybees."

Don't become so well-adjusted to your culture that you fit into it without even thinking. Instead, fix your attention on God. You'll be changed from the inside out. Readily recognize what he wants from you, and quickly respond to it. Unlike the culture around you, always dragging you down to its level of immaturity, God brings the best out of you, develops well-formed maturity in you.

ROMANS 12:2

Prayer is always an act of faith. It begins with faith, must be carried through in faith, and finished in faith. Every ordinary prayer prayed in the most ordinary way by the most ordinary person is a revolutionary statement of trust.

MEL LAWRENZ
PATTERNS

Fulfillment
the sweetest spot

Your life has a plot; your years have a theme. You can do something in a manner that no one else can. And when you find it and do it, another sweet spot is discovered.

MAX LUCADO
CURE FOR THE COMMON LIFE

Author and storyteller Max Lucado has created an acronym for discovering our "sweet spot," that is, our God-given inclination toward excellence in a particular area, an inherent ability, a certain knack for a specific task, a wonderful born-with-it talent resting deep inside every one of us, just waiting for the opportunity to shine. That sweet spot may manifest itself in those subtle stirrings of inner longing we experience when we observe the gifts of others or it may come to us in casual conversation anywhere, anytime. All it takes is self-awareness and the desire to share our innate gifts and talents. Discovering our sweet spot can bring both personal satisfaction and the blessing of seeing that gift spill over to the people in our lives.

Lucado uses *S.T.O.R.Y.* to guide the process of self-discovery, to help us find a match for our gifts. We must first identify our *strengths* by bringing to mind things we've done well in the past. Next, we need to determine what types of objects we enjoy working with. In other words, we need to identify *topics* of interest. We also need to discover the *optimal* conditions that incite personal passion and excitement. For example, do we pour ourselves into challenges involving people or are we task-oriented? A brief *relationship* examination can help us discover how we function best, for example, working alone or in a group. Finally, we need to find that specific job, task, vocation or goal that rouses our inner *"Yes!"* and take practical steps to achieve it.

As more of us learn to accurately recognize our own "sweet spots," our families and the entire community will reap the benefits. What could be better than a family, church, community or world full of people doing what we were made to do and loving every minute of it!

MAX LUCADO'S GUIDE FOR FINDING YOUR SWEET SPOT

- S — Discover personal **strengths.**
- T — Find your desired **topic.**
- O — Locate the **optimal conditions.**
- R — Consider **relationships.**
- Y — Find that inner **"Yes!"**

Peace

"God's raging anger won't let up
until he's made a clean sweep
completing the job he began.
When the job's done
you'll see it's been well done."

JEREMIAH 30:24

Rarely do we identify fighting for something — a cause, a belief, a person — as an act of peace. But biblically speaking, there is nothing more peaceable than fighting for what is right. Whether we witness an injustice or are in a position to offer relief and comfort to someone who's been injured or wronged, there is no more loving choice than to summon our courage and get involved. Make no mistake about it, getting involved in the messiness of the life of another life takes immense courage and inner resolve.

Unfortunately, even with the best of intentions, we can be easily misunderstood, misconstrued or even rejected when we offer love and support. It's the risk we take. It's the risk God *expects* us to take. Prayerfully, thoughtfully, peaceably, we enter into the lives of those around us, always with their best interests at heart. May God give us both the wisdom, the desire and the discernment to act as Jesus' loving ambassadors of hope.

High Alert

Janet bent over and pulled with all her might. She knew better. She *really* did. But it didn't budge. Instead of falling flat on her hindquarters, as she had the week before, she gave in to the stubborn rhubarb plant and went for her knife.

Minutes later, Janet stacked a mound of rhubarb next to the outside faucet and washed off the worst of the soil that clung to the stalks. She shook her head and chuckled, "Not a fast learner, eh?" She recounted all the other times she'd forgotten to tote her handy garden tools to the garden, having to improvise in order to plant, weed or harvest her vegetables and flowers.

Shaking the remaining debris free, she took her bounty inside and washed it once more before cutting the hardy stalks into three-quarter-inch slices. In no time she had enough for three pies. "Yum," she said in anticipation. Just then the phone rang, breaking her pleasant reverie.

Janet dried her hands and reached for the portable extension. It was Marie, one of Janet's oldest friends, the one and only friend who could exhaust her faster than any friend or family member. Talking with Marie was like being thrust into warp speed and then suddenly dropped midair — kerplunk — onto the pavement. Sad, but oh so true.

While Janet truly loved Marie, she found that coaxing Marie out of her constant emotional funks depleted all her energy. Over the years she had tried to get Marie to see that life wasn't all death and disaster, but she had given up. It wasn't even Marie's negativity that dampened Janet's spirit and drove her to the brink. It was Marie's intensity.

As Janet stood at her kitchen counter, trying to make her favorite seasonal treat, she suppressed her irritation and tried to listen. Marie started detailing her reasons for going back to college for her master's degree. Before long, Janet wasn't really listening anymore. Instead she was focusing on her recipe.

Marie must have sensed her lack of attention. "What are you busy with today?' Marie queried.

Janet explained, "Making rhubarb pies from the recipe you gave me, Marie. It's the best one I've ever eaten!"

"Thanks," Marie gushed, adding, "And Janet, thanks for listening. I know I'm pretty obsessive sometimes, but having you around really helps."

Hanging up, Janet stood for a moment contemplating the parallels between her own willfulness with the rhubarb plant earlier in the day and Marie's insistence that life conform to her expectations. "We may not exhibit it outwardly," Janet had to admit, "but I guess Marie and I aren't so different after all."

Every part of Scripture is God-breathed and useful one way or another — showing us truth, exposing our rebellion, correcting our mistakes, training us to live God's way. Through the Word we are put together and shaped up for the tasks God has for us.

2 TIMOTHY 3:16-17

Ambassadors need to speak with an understanding of the King's methods. An ambassador is called not only to say what the King would say, but to say it in the way he would say it.

PAUL DAVID TRIPP
WAR OF WORDS

Peace

intervening with love

> *I know that every good and excellent thing in the world stands moment by moment on the razor-edge of danger and must be fought for...."*
> Thornton Wilder
> *The Skin of Our Teeth*

What thoughts come to mind when you think about making peace with someone? Often our first impressions may be a painful mix of tense, disagreeable memories and emotionally charged exchanges. Instinctively, we stiffen. We resist the notion that it just may be *our* responsibility to take the lead in seeking pardon. No doubt about it, pursuing peace can be a gutsy, courageous endeavor. It's also a journey to be undertaken with great forethought and care, a journey rarely taken without some personal sacrifice.

One type of peacemaking — *intervention*, also known as *restoration* — involves interceding for the well-being of another. It is an act of true friendship, an expression of genuine concern. We all need at least one other person brave enough to take on this role for us if and when we need it. This kind of peacemaking requires internal fortitude to face risks many of us are unwilling to take. The risk of rejection. Loss of relationship. Misunderstanding. Accusation and recrimination. Even so, the pursuit of peace is not up for debate. Peacemaking is absolutely essential. It can even save lives.

Unfortunately, we might assume that peace — even peace at any price — is the end goal, but this approach to peace is shortsighted at best. Simply keeping quiet over a difficult and potentially destructive matter may seem like a way to keep the peace, but it just does not cut it.

What does real peacemaking look like when someone you care for is addicted to drugs, alcohol, overspending, career or another obsession? According to Ken Sande, author of *The Peacemaker*, peacemakers are able to see the long-term effects of another's damaging actions and attitudes. They must be willing to take several proactive steps to offer a healthier way. Sande writes that peacemaking includes speaking conversationally with someone by "encouraging self-control, asking questions, clarifying facts and offering tangible help." The purpose is always to draw a person back from a place of danger. This is the kind of peacemaking we must champion, protect and nurture. Let's face it. We all need others to help us make peace with those things we are unable to either let go of — or take hold of — on our own. Life can be a battle. Let's fight for one another…peaceably.

Learning to Fight for Peace

- Define the word *peace*. Recognize that being peaceable often means gentle confrontation out of concern for what is best for another person.
- Define the long-term goal of peace. Realize that working through difficult personal issues frequently takes time. During that in-between period, tension might be part of the process.
- Define what it looks like to be a peacemaker and the person in need of peace. Learn to initiate peacemaking and learn to humbly accept help and instruction when you are the one in need.

Sources

Andrews, Andy. *The Traveler's Gift*. Nashville, TN: Thomas Nelson Publishers, 2002.

Brown, H. Jackson, Jr., and Rosemary C. Brown. *Life's Little Instructions from the Bible*. Nashville, TN: Rutledge Hill Press, 2000.

Chambers, Oswald. *My Utmost for His Highest*. Grand Rapids, MI: Discovery House Publishers, 1992.

Curtis, Brent, and John Eldredge. *The Sacred Romance*. Nashville, TN: Thomas Nelson, 1997.

Editors. *God's Little Devotional Journal for Women*. Tulsa, OK: Honor Books, 2000.

Edwards, Dwight. *Releasing the Rivers Within*. Colorado Springs, CO: WaterBrook Press, 2003.

Ireland, David. *Secrets of a Satisfied Life*. Ada, MI: Baker Books, 2006.

Lawrenz, Mel. *Patterns*. Grand Rapids, MI: Zondervan, 2003.

Lucado, Max. *Cure for the Common Life*. Nashville, TN: Thomas Nelson, 2005.

McKinley, David H. *The Search for Satisfaction: Looking for Something New Under the Sun*. Nashville, TN: W Publishing Group, 2006.

Phillips, Michael. *Make Me Like Jesus*. Colorado Springs, CO: WaterBrook Press, 2003.

Swindoll, Charles R. *Strengthening Your Grip*. Waco, TX: Word Books, 1982.

Swindoll, Luci. *I Married Adventure*. Nashville, TN: W Publishing Group, 2003.

Tibbits, Dick. *Forgive to Live: How Forgiveness Can Save Your Life.* Nashville, TN: Thomas Nelson, 2008.

Tripp, Paul David. *War of Words.* Phillipsburg, New Jersey: P & R Publishing, 2000.

Warren Rick. *The Purpose Driven Life.* Grand Rapids, MI: Zondervan, 2002.

Welch, Edward T. *When People Are Big and God Is Small.* Phillipsburg, NJ: P & R Publishing, 1997.

White, James. Emery. *Life-Defining Moments.* Colorado Springs, CO: WaterBrook Press, 2001.

White, Jerry. *Making Peace With Reality.* Colorado Springs, CO: NavPress, 2002.

Whitney, Donald S. *Simplify Your Spiritual Life.* Colorado Springs, CO: NavPress, 2003.

Wilhite, Jud. *Faith That Goes the Distance.* Grand Rapids, MI: Baker Books, 2002.